CENTRAL BRITTANY

Coast to Coast

Things to see and do in the heart of Brittany, including 12 walks with maps and directions

by

Penny Allen

with drawings by the author

Central Brittany: Coast to Coast
published by Red Dog Books
ISBN 0 9536001 6 5

To Ismay

British Library Cataloguing-in-Publication Data
A catalogue record for this book is available from the British Library

Red Dog Books is based in Axbridge, Somerset and in Brittany.
Enquiries should be addressed to the editorial office at
Red Dog Books, 29410 Plounéour-Ménez, France.

email: reddogbooks@tiscali.fr

www.reddogbooks.com

Printed and bound in China

Front Cover: Josselin (main), Liscuis, Morieux, Lac de Guerlédan
Back Cover: Le Val-André (top), Malestroit, Dahouët

ABOUT THIS BOOK

The purpose of this book is to introduce the reader to the central region of Brittany, comprising the majority of the departments of Côtes d'Armor and Morbihan. To the west of this region lies Finistère, while to the east are Ille-et-Villaine and Loire Atlantique. Together these five departments make up the area of Brittany as it has been known through the centuries.

SECTION A The book divides **central Brittany** into 6 areas (see map on page 4). Each of these is covered separately with its own detailed map and an alphabetic arrangement of things to see and do. An idea of distances can be gained from the examples given on the maps and with this information, excursions to selected places can be planned from any given starting point. The key to enjoyment is not to be in a hurry. It is hoped that the recommendations in this book will lead each visitor to further discoveries of their own.

SECTION B For closer exploration of the countryside, the book also contains 12 numbered walks, with maps and full directions, spread throughout central Brittany. Their locations are marked and numbered on the maps.

SECTION C These reference listings include key information arranged under specific topics to enable visitors to pursue a particular line of interest.

ABOUT THE AUTHOR

Penny Allen has published numerous articles in magazines and newspapers as diverse as Cosmopolitan, the Guardian, Caduceus, Time Out and the Times.

For many years she ran a practice and courses in healing and astrology, and an earlier book, The Face of the Deep, explores the influence of the planets on our lives.

Since 1997 she has lived in the heart of Brittany, renovating an ancient village with a manor house, cottages and a forge.

MAP OF CENTRAL BRITTANY

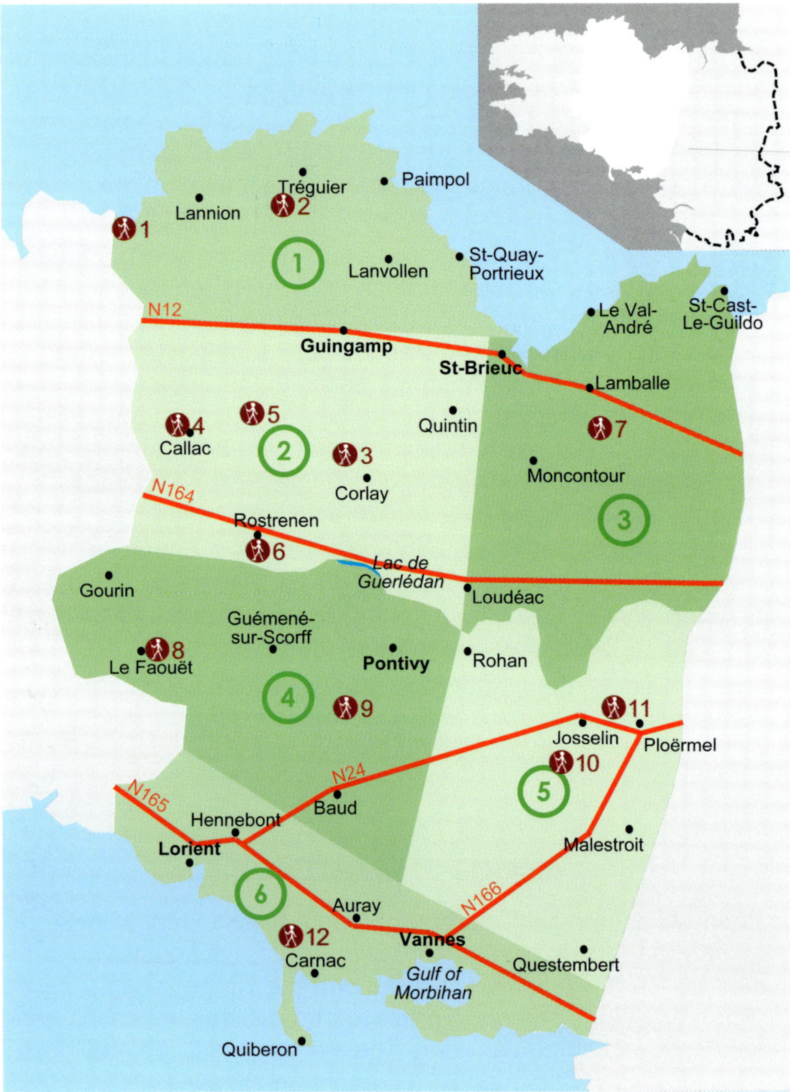

1 AREAS for SECTION A - Places of Interest

1 WALKS for SECTION B

CONTENTS

GLOSSARY

argoat = the wooded interior
armor = land of the sea
balisage = waymarking for walks
boucle = circuit
chaos = rocks in a river valley
Chouans/Chouannerie = anti-revolutionary movement
douanier = customs officer
fest noz = evening/night festival
fest deiz = daytime festival
fontaine/feunteun = spring or fountain
plan d'eau = reservoir, artificial lake
sentier = footpath
ville fleurie = town of flowers
ville close = walled town

ABBREVIATIONS & SYMBOLS

TO = Tourist Office

GR = Grande Randonnée (national long distance footpath - marked with red and white slash)

◆ = highly recommended

1 = walk

Walk Map symbols

✧ archaeological or historical feature
✳ belvedere/viewpoint
▬ building(s)
campsite
château
church or chapel
† calvary or wayside cross
fontaine/spring
dolmen
menhir
P parking
2 refers to a point in the written directions

NB: On area maps, places not mentioned in the text are shown in grey.

INTRODUCTION

Kreizh Breizh, or Central Brittany, is blessed with two long and winding coastlines of rocky coves, wide sandy beaches, dramatic cliffs and a sea studded with islands. In the north the Emerald coast and Pink Granite coast are renowned for their startlingly coloured and weirdly-shaped boulders and in the south the remarkable Gulf of Morbihan is said to have an island for every day of the year. North and south, sleepy harbours are interspersed with lively resorts. Inland, the green hills and valleys, streams, forests and rivers offer a treasure trove of exploratory delights.

©RDB

Though it has, over the centuries, absorbed French customs and culture, Brittany remains fiercely Breton and the conscious attempt during the latter part of the twentieth century to keep the culture alive has born fruit. The Breton language, still spoken by choice by the older generation, is now once again taught in schools and one radio channel is devoted to Breton music and language. Breton dance, too, has survived and the dancers who perform at the 'fest deiz' and 'fest noz' – daytime and night festivals – are dressed in the traditional formal black costumes with lace hats and collars that have been passed through the generations. The festivals, though welcoming visitors, are by no means geared to tourism and are as popular as they have ever been with the local people, who flock to listen to their popular heroes and heroines, among them the Frères Morvan, three brothers now in their eighties and still living together in their natal home in the heart of Brittany, who learned to sing from their mother.

Brittany is and always has been a hard working, agricultural place, exposed to the elements on sea and land, and the Breton people have far too much to do to devote themselves to tourism. This is what makes Brittany such an attractive place to visit: though holidays may include water-sports, golf, fishing, walking, cycling and much besides, there is always more to do, investigating the past and the present of the land and culture, which has been formed over the centuries by invasion upon invasion, from Celts and Romans to Saxons, English and Germans and, not least, the French.

To visit a small village can be just as illuminating as to explore a town, the local history most easily accessible through the church and the contemporary culture through the bar. Many villages have a history that can be traced back to Neolithic times and can be explored through the surrounding land where ancient stone sites, tumuli and mottes may still stand.

Though mid-Brittany has few large, sprawling cities, it does contain many smaller towns, often fortified and still giving a strong sense of the traditional way of life. To stroll around their alleys and streets marvelling at the architecture and calling in at their châteaux, abbeys, churches and monasteries is to become a part of the rich and intense history chronicling the power and later demise of the great dukedoms, the overthrow of the aristocracy and, of course, the loss of the autonomy of Brittany to its French neighbour, while visits to the disused mills, some now museums, give a fascinating education in the story of the linen trade which made Brittany wealthy in later years.

It is due, they say, to the traditional independence of the Breton peninsula that there are no road tolls here and yet the roads are every bit as good as elsewhere in France and getting around is easy. Sadly, the canal that runs the width of the peninsula from Nantes to Brest is used today for leisure purposes only: the tow path provides easy walking and cycling and the rivers and lakes (many of them reservoirs) give opportunities for sailing and canoeing, while the two coastlines provide plenty of activities for the energetic and, for the less active, abundant opportunities to do absolutely nothing at all.

Penny Allen

©RDB

ACKNOWLEDGEMENTS

The author would like to thank H. Mewes and J. Smith for their contributions to the Morbihan coverage in this book.

Photographs are in most cases from the Red Dog Books archives (©RDB). Those by the author are marked ©PA, and those by Judy Smith ©JS.

All drawings are by the author

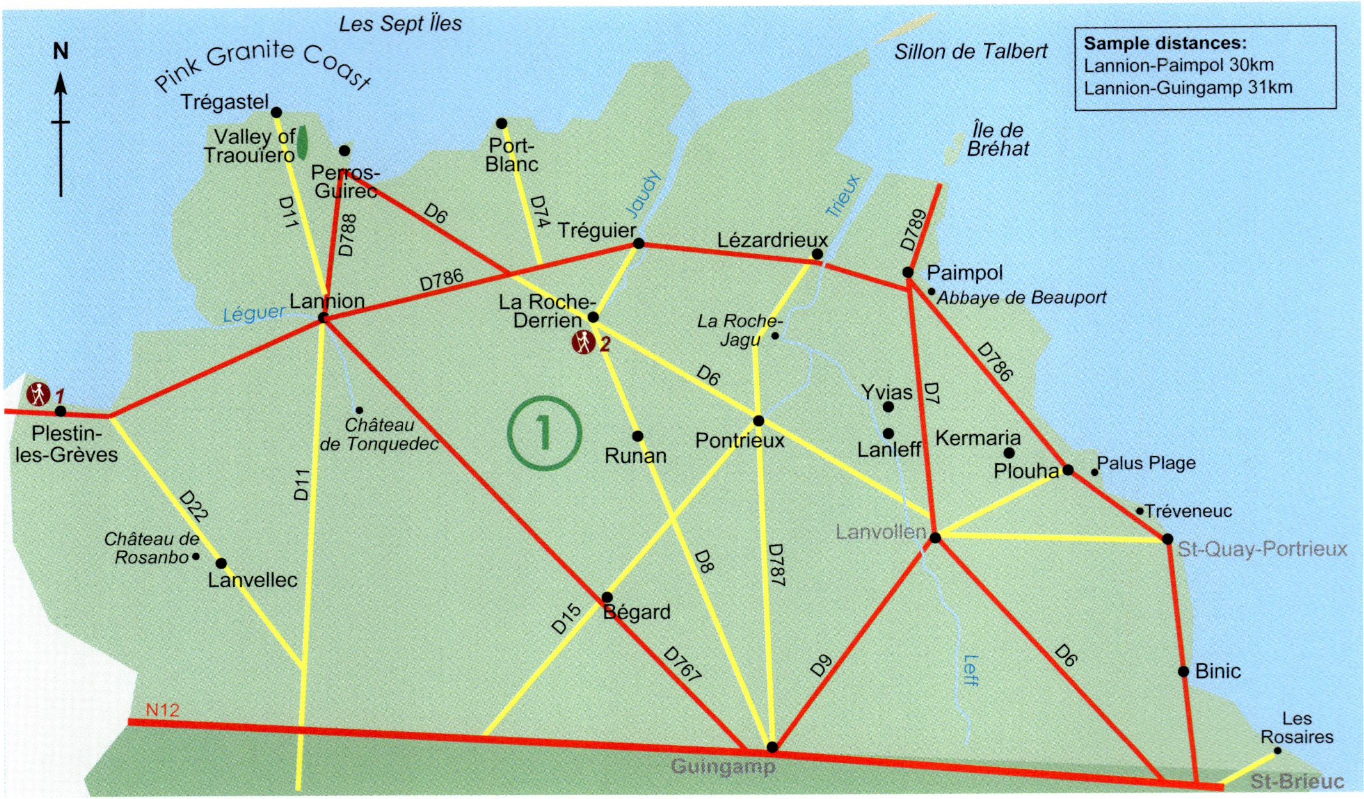

Sample distances:
Lannion-Paimpol 30km
Lannion-Guingamp 31km
N
Les Sept Îles
Pink Granite Coast
Sillon de Talbert
Île de Bréhat
Trégastel
Valley of Traouïero
Perros-Guirec
Port-Blanc
Tréguier
Jaudy
Lézardrieux
Trieux
Paimpol
Abbaye de Beauport
Lannion
Léguer
La Roche-Derrien
La Roche-Jagu
Plestin-les-Grèves
Château de Tonquedec
Runan
Pontrieux
Yvias
Lanleff
Kermaria
Plouha
Palus Plage
Tréveneuc
Lanvollen
St-Quay-Portrieux
Château de Rosanbo
Lanvellec
Bégard
Leff
Binic
Les Rosaires
Guingamp
St-Brieuc
N12
D11
D788
D6
D74
D786
D789
D7
D22
D15
D767
D8
D787
D9
1
2

SECTION A

1. The Northern Coast and its hinterland from Plestin-Les-Grèves to St-Brieuc

This is an area with much to offer in addition to its exceptional coastline, which provides an earthly paradise for walkers and beach-lovers alike. The interior is full of colourful and picturesque estuary towns, such as Lannion, Tréguier and the exquisite Pontrieux, as well as enticing river valleys at every turn. Notable also is the wealth of religious buildings from the enigmatic Temple to the well-named Abbey de Beauport and the rich decoration of chapels such as Kermaria.

Abbaye de Beauport

♦ ABBAYE de BEAUPORT

Founded by Count Alain de Penthièvre et de Goëlo in 1202 for monks from Mont St-Michel and Avranches, the abbey, on a coastal site which is not only beautiful but strategic, was once a seat of great power and authority. Remains of the chapter house, cloisters and refectory can still be seen. The abbey was sold as 'Bien national' during the Revolution and is today owned by the Conservatoire du Littoral which protects the largely ruined abbey and its grounds, containing a rose garden, cider apple orchards and a little sheltered port.

It is open every day throughout the year and gives courses in the cultivation of apples and the history of the abbey. In season there are guided outings into the countryside including night walks on Wednesdays and Sundays, a festival of old plants in July and concerts on Thursday evenings in summer. Booking is advised: 02 96 55 18 58

BEGARD

The best thing in Brittany, in some small people's minds, is situated at Bégard: **Amoripark** (02 96 45 36 36). This swimming and activity centre is open every day in summer and at other times throughout the year. It may well be some larger people's idea of hell!

©RDB

The historical remains around Bégard span thousands of years: from the menhir of Kergwezhenneg and the feudal motte of Pont Niou to the 15th century chapel of Botlezan and the dovecote of Kernaudour with its thousand pigeon-holes dating from the 16th/17th century.

Well-marked walks around Bégard criss-cross the valleys of the Trieux and the Jaudy and their tributaries. Start at Armoripark to walk either 4 or 7 kms along the valley of the Donant, or take the 8km walk along the Trieux starting in front of the church at Tregonneau (where you can also visit the menhir of Kerbour and the Dolmen de Beuzit). There is a 10km circuit of the valley of the Perrier starting at Kermoroc'h, or you can simply walk around the lake at Poullogwer, which used to belong to the abbey of Bégard.

BINIC (TO 02 96 73 60 12)

The charming port of Binic is a pleasure to stroll around, admiring the boats and the old narrow streets. The **Museum of Popular Traditions**, in a former canning factory, displays items relating to Binic's history as an important cod-fishing port and agricultural centre. Watch the sun go down over dinner in one of the numerous cafés offering good value food at outdoor tables.

Île de BREHAT (TO 02 96 20 04 15)

Take the ferry (02 96 55 79 50) from the Pointe de l'Arcouest at Paimpol to the Isle of Brehat, two miles long and one mile wide. Very like the Scilly Isles, the warm climate permits the cultivation of exotic as well as native plants some of which spring from the sun-drenched walls of the cottages sprinkled over what are actually two linked islands.

Bréhat's rocky coast ©PA

The little town, le Bourg, is packed with visitors in summer but a pleasure to sit around in, and the car-free island is heaven to explore. Rent bikes at the ferry port, have a tennis tournament in the courts behind the town, explore the wild, northern end of the island, climb the rocks along the coast, take a dip in the sea and feed on oysters and chips.

(From l'Arcouest a short ferry trip also goes up the Trieux past Lézardrieux, and day trips go to Erquy and Binic.)

KERMARIA see PLOUHA

LANLEFF see YVIAS

◆ **LANNION** (TO 02 96 46 41 00)

The heart of Lannion is chic, old and fascinating, despite the town's reputation in the development of telecommunications. Market on a Thursday sprawls over the car park by the River Léguer and up the cobbled street that rises to a square of medieval houses, on the corner of which is a traditional bakery where you, like everything else, may get a dusting of flour when you call in to see the bread being cooked in the wood-fired oven.

Lannion ©RDB

The hill continues to mount to another square and the 142 steps leading up to the church of Brelevenez (Hill of Joy) with its magnificent views. It has been surmised that the foundation was a Templar one, by the soldier-monks of Montjoie, but others see it as a Trinitarian church. The earliest parts are Romanesque and the crypt can be visited.

Take a boat trip on the river (02 96 37 23 48) or cross it and drive along the left bank to the peninsula with good cliff walks and little beaches, or walk up either river bank to the sea.

LANVELLEC

Though the road runs through Lanvellec dividing the church from the rest, it has a calm, clear atmosphere. Walks all round it reveal a wealth of history and the GR long-distance footpath passes through. For the autumn festival each year the village takes on a very convincing air of the past, the roofs covered in temporary thatch and straw strewn all over the roads with not a car in sight. The villagers dress as of yesteryear in clothes that tell us of their status and even their occupation, and process, some on foot, some on horse-drawn carts, down the main street to the church, singing, dancing and playing musical instruments. Also in autumn, an organ festival of mainly Baroque music is held in the church.

The nearby **Château de Rosanbo**, at the end of its long tree-lined drive, is typical of its period (17th-19th century) with a large dovecote and formally laid-out gardens. These were designed by famous landscape gardener Achille Duchene (who made a water garden at Blenheim palace) in the early 20th century, and are a pleasure to walk around.

LEZARDRIEUX

Once a major port for shipping to England, Lézardrieux has little of its former glory but is an attractive small town with a harbour, walks along the Trieux and views out to the lighthouse. Market day is Friday.

PAIMPOL (TO 02 96 20 83 16)

©RDB

A lot cheaper than the much-publicised La Vapeur du Trieux steam train that runs from Paimpol to Pontrieux and back (02 96 95 14 03) is the ordinary, very sweet, train that goes along the same magnificent track from Guingamp to Paimpol.

Once a major fishing port, Paimpol is now dominated by sailing boats and the character of the old harbours has gone. But visitors can go out for half a day at sea in *le Vieux Copain*, attend the festivals of sea shanties in the summer and visit the **Musée de la Mer** (sea museum) to find out about the town's 500 year fishing history in the icy waters of Newfoundland and Iceland. There is also a tiny **Musée du Costume** displaying clothes and furniture from Brittany's past. Market day is Tuesday.

PALUS PLAGE

An easy drive from Plouha takes you to the car park at the sandy beach of Palus. The sea here is pleasantly swimmable though still within striking distance of the conurbation of St-Brieuc. There are caves and cliffs to explore, whilst behind the beach is a children's playground and the woods offer a variety of walks. Canoes and other seaside delights can be hired (Centre d'Activités Nautiques du Goëlo Argoat give lessons too: 02 96 22 62 66) and there are good cafés and a well-situated but discreet hotel.

Climb the steep steps next to the Café Homardine (a good place to eat local fish as well as to admire the exotic ones in the fish tanks) to the cliff top for superb views and to walk on to Pointe de Plouha and Gwin Zegal.

©PA

PERROS-GUIREC (TO 02 96 23 21 15)

Perros-Guirec presents itself as the Monte Carlo of the North Coast, offering a casino, a marina and thalossotherapy among its attractions. But it is hard to imagine that this sturdily Breton town could fool anyone, pleasant enough though it is for a visit and to set off for the coast or for a boat trip to the Sept Îles.

The **Musée de Cire** (waxworks) portrays the horrendous events precipitated by the French Revolution and the anti-revolutionary Catholic movement (Chouannerie) of the late 18th century. The Federation of Traditional Breton Fêtes, 02 96 49 08 92, gives information on fêtes in Perros-Guirec and elsewhere. Market day is Friday.

©JS

♦THE PINK GRANITE COAST

The Pink Granite Coast, stretching from Bréhat to Trégastel, emerged from the sea some 130,000 years ago, its weathered rocks forming extraordinary shapes, many with evocative names such as Napoleon's Hat, the Rabbit and the Death's Head. The granite is said to have got its colour from the blood of persecuted saints. The most dramatic area is between Perros-Guirec and Ploumanac'h where wonderful walks on the reasonably flat coast studded with massive boulders offer children plenty to explore. The coastal path is the Sentier des Douaniers, formerly patrolled by customs officers on the lookout for smugglers. The most astonishing of the rocks of the Pink Granite Coast are to be found at Ploumanac'h. From Pors-Kamor cove and Ploumanac'h lighthouse the view to the Sept Îles is stunning.

PLESTIN-les-GREVES (TO 02 96 35 61 93)

The Sunday morning market at Plestin-les-Grèves must surely be the best in Côtes d'Armor. Here you can browse for items of interest, stock up with a wide variety of provisions or simply soak up the relaxed atmosphere.

Nearby is the leisure centre of Etang de Mesqueau, horse riding at Kerropartz near St-Michel-en-Grève and a bat reservation at le Grand Rocher near St-Efflam.

Ask at the tourist office or mairie for information about the archaeological digs that are often underway nearby. The Thermes du Hogolo, remains of a Roman bath on the Douron estuary, were only excavated in the 1980s. (See Walk No.1, page 84)

PLOUHA (TO 02 96 20 24 73)

Though only a few kilometres from the sea, Plouha retains a refreshing atmosphere of serious daily business, scarcely giving the time of day to passing tourists. The main square has a number of good bars and a lively market on Wednesdays. Art exhibitions are held at Castel Pic (02 96 20 27 10) and more art can be seen in the rue des Frères Leguen.

A visit to the 'Sept Chapelles' can be arranged on 02 96 20 35 78. This will include the fabulous ◆**Chapel of Kermaria** with its famous frescoes, or just visit this chapel in summer when it is open all day. It dates originally from the 13th century, although its most remarkable features are later. The porch has a little hall of records above and an external balcony for delivering judgments. At entry level, it contains painted wooden statues of the twelve apostles. The 15th century colourful frescoes in the nave show the fascinating Danse Macabre or Dance of Death – 47 medieval figures of varied social standing linked by what they all have in common: death. (See also the church at Kernascléden, page 54.)

Chapel of Kermaria ©RDB

◆**PONTRIEUX** (TO 02 96 95 14 03)

'Pontrieux, coin delicieux', goes an old song and the town certainly knows how to make the most of its assets: floral decorations cover its pretty bridge while the lavoirs along the river banks, where until recently women washed their clothes, are now a tourist attraction with a special festival, the fête des Lavandières, in mid-August. It is a centre for crafts with a stained-glass window maker and several art galleries.

Take a boat trip along the river at night (book at the tourist office) and visit the little park by the river by day. North of the main town, walk up the right bank of the river past the little harbour, stopping at the crêperie for a snack. Or take a 5km walk along the Trieux starting at the tourist office, unmistakeable in its medieval house on the main through road.

Pontrieux ©PA

PORT BLANC (TO 02 96 92 81 09)

Anatole Braz, the renowned collector of local Breton legends, described the sea at Port Blanc as 'divine, the swimming isles clothed in light'. A simple, even humble little port, it has, nonetheless, attracted its share of celebrities including Marie Curie. It has also attracted the English both in war and peace since at least 1230, when they helped to finance the Bretons against the French. Situated on the vulnerable headland, the chapel at Port Blanc was originally a 'tour de garde', a watch tower looking out to sea.

Walk the coastal path to le Royo and back with its view of the Île aux Femmes and Île Saint-Gildas, where a chapel has stood since the 11th century or, to make a circular walk, return via the calvary at Crec'h André and Poulpri. The 'école de voile' (sailing school) at Port Blanc gives lessons in sailing, canoeing and fishing and the *Ausqueme* sailing boat takes visitors out for fishing and bird-watching trips.

The market is on Saturday.

♦La ROCHE-DERRIEN

(TO 02 96 91 50 22)

La Roche-Derrien is situated on a rocky hill above the river Jaudy, where it widens into mudflats, attracting a variety of birds (including white herons) on its way to the sea. In the central square a number of medieval timber-framed houses still stand, sagging somewhat but looking solid enough to last another few centuries. (See Walk No.2, page 87)

La Roche-Derrien ©PA

Château de la ROCHE-JAGU (02 96 95 62 35)

Built in 1405, vertiginously high above the River Trieux, the château is now civic-owned and has been renovated. Inside, the château is fascinating with its numerous fireplaces and surprisingly airy spaces. The his-and-hers chapel is charming and the walks along the upper corridors give a magnificent view of the winding, muddy Trieux and the wooded bank opposite.

Three walks around the land are indicated on the map in the car park but it is just as good to find your own way round the herb and rose gardens, camellia walks, wisteria tunnels and down to the little harbour. The château often houses art exhibitions and in summer the public can attend lively, good-humoured, free spectacles on the lawns.

Les ROSAIRES

Unusual among the beaches of the north coast, Les Rosaires is not only easily accessible but has a Mediterranean feel with its flat sands arrived at by walking through a busy complex of cafés and souvenir shops and its array of children's activities on the beach, including trampolining.

RUNAN

For a small place, Runan has a remarkably richly decorated church, with many elements from the 15th and 16th centuries, including a fine altarpiece and stained-glass window of the Crucifixion. It benefited from the patronage and largesse of the Templars and the Duke of Brittany as well as lords from the Château of Roche-Jagu. There is also an ossuary and an outdoor pulpit.

Armorials set in the church walls ©RDB

Les SEPT ILES

The boat trip round the seven islands only stops in good weather on the Île aux Moines, named after the monks who tried to colonise it. Otherwise it is purely an ornithological event, the islands having offered protection to birds, including puffins, gannets, cormorants, kittiwakes and fulmars, since 1912, although nothing could have protected them from the disastrous oil slick that drenched the Pink Granite Coast in 1967. Seals can also sometimes be seen. Reservations: 02 96 23 22 47.

♦SILLON de TALBERT

This extraordinary geological feature, a three kilometre long spit of sand and pebbles projecting from the point between the rivers Jaudy and Trieux, somehow manages to hold its own against the Channel tides. It is possible to walk right out along it, except in nesting season as it is a haven for sea-birds.

avocet

Château de TONQUEDEC

Situated boldly on a low promontory overlooking the river Léguer, this medieval walled castle seems to be asking for trouble. And it has certainly had it. It was destroyed twice before being rebuilt and massively fortified for the Crusader Roland IV of Coëtmen in the 15th century, but then once again largely dismantled in the early 17th century on Cardinal Richelieu's order, after supporters of Marie de Medicis, who had seized the castle, were defeated. The castle is open for visits in season.

©RDB

Château de Tonquedec

Valley of TRAOUIERO

This site is actually two parallel valleys of exceptional beauty and natural interest. The name means 'Valley of the Valley' – the map-makers of Louis XIVth not being familiar with the Breton language. Information boards give details of walking trails among the granite chaos, caves and unusual vegetation. A cool place to visit on a hot summer's day!

TREGASTEL (TO 02 96 15 38 38)

There is plenty to do and visit here, including the recently-built swimming pool overlooking the beach at Coz-Porz, the **Radôme** telecommunications centre at Pleumeur-Bodou (02 96 46 63 80), with museums, scientific games and a 'virtual world', and the **Planetarium Côte de Granit Rose** (02 96 15 80 32).

The menhir at St-Uzec is also worth a short detour for its impressive size and unusual decoration thanks to Christianisation in the 17th century. As well as a cross added to the top, there is elaborate carving of the instruments of Christ's passion, and a moon and sun to symbolise death and resurrection.

Christianised menhir ©RDB

♦TREGUIER

(TO 02 96 92 23 33)

Statue of Ernest Renan ©RDB

Tréguier is bursting with history and it is easy to trace the conflict between its Catholic hierarchy and its dissidents, most notably the historian of religion, Ernest Renan, whose faith was undermined by his studies of linguistics and metaphysics. He was a renowned thinker and the author of many important books such as The Life of Jesus and a history of the origins of Christianity. His modern statue, protected by the goddess of justice, sits defiantly in the cathedral square and his timber-framed childhood home is now a museum (02 96 93 45 63).

Tréguier cathedral ©RDB

The **Cathedral of St-Tugdual** is also the centre of worship of Brittany's own St-Yves, who was born near here in 1253. He was a lawyer and judge of exceptional honesty and fairness, before deciding to change his life by becoming a priest and ministering to the poor. Miracles associated with his ministry led to a cult centring on his relics and tomb in the cathedral where he was buried. The tomb today is a copy of one dedicated to St-Yves in the 15th century by the Duke of Brittany, and there is also a fine early statue of the saint.

Next to the pretentious calvary opposite the river (erected in protest at the honouring of Renan) a gateway leads into a tranquil park with a children's play area and a variety of trees displaying their French names. Another open space, le Bois du Poète, which borders a branch of the river Jaudy, provides space for camper cars and a pleasant walk along the river front to an old cobbled bridge, now closed.

TREVENEUC

Tréveneuc, with its beautiful church and massive decaying château with grounds stretching to the sea, still retains its grandeur. The Château de Pommorio was built in 1780 and nearby are the remains of an early 15th century fort.

Park at Port Goret and snack in the simple café on the cliff but, instead of swimming in the less-than-pristine waters here, walk the cliff path to Palus Plage.

©PA

Dovecote of the Château de Pommorio

YVIAS and LANLEFF

The secluded 'bourg' of Yvias, perched on a hill and often in cloud, has the air of an Alpine village. Breakfast on coffee and croissants with a newspaper to hand in the friendly café and then set out for one of a number of walks through the forests and along the river. From here, you can walk to Lanleff which is on the GR footpath leading to the coastal path and surrounded by a number of shorter paths. It is ideal to arrive at Lanleff on foot and to visit its ruined temple which looks, at first sight, to be Roman, but is now thought to have been built in the 11th century on the design of the Church of the Holy Sepulchre in Jerusalem.

Temple at Lanleff ©PA

COMMENTS

The river Leff, one of the most beautiful in Côtes d'Armor, is particularly attractive south-west of Lanvollen. La Roche-Derrien is a gem, with perfect architecture and great river walks in both directions and, for coastal walks, nothing can beat the cliffs north of Palus Plage.

A negative note, however, in an exceptionally beautiful area: the extensive renovations to the buildings and land at the civic-owned Roche-Jagu have entailed considerable destruction and the loss of a personal touch. Insensitivity can also be seen at Tréveneuc, where the grandeur conveyed by the church and the château is now under attack from the ugly holiday homes sprouting up with no concern for heritage or aesthetics.

St-Brieuc
Châtelaudren
Quintin
Guingamp
Plouisy
Grâces
Menez-Bré
Bourbriac
St-Fiacre
Corlay
Kerpert
Lanrivain
St-Nicolas-du-Pelem
Plussulien
Ste-Trephine
Laniscat
Liscuis
Gorges du Daoulas
Rosquelfen
Gouarec
Abbaye de Bon Repos
Lac de Guerlédan
Blavet
Mûr-de-Bretagne
St-Guen
St-Thélo
Loudéac
D700
D790
D7
D767
D8
D787
D44
D33
D11
N12
N164
La Chêne de Tronjoly
Pestivien
Bulat-Pestivien
Coat-Maël
Gorges de Toul-Goulic
Kergrist-Moëlou
Rostrenen
Glomel
Gorges du Corong
Locarn
Maël-Carhaix
Callac
Belle-Isle-en-Terre
Plougonver
Loguivy-Plougras
Forêt de Beffou
Carhaix-Plouguer
Nantes-Brest Canal
Gourin
Sample distances:
Guingamp - Corlay 28km
Rostrenen - St-Brieuc 59km
N
2
3
4
5
6

2. The Argoat of Côtes D'Armor southwest of St-Brieuc

There are few settlements of any size in this heart of central Brittany, where quiet little villages with their simple churches and chapels nestle among the wooded hills.The Argoat is a scene of wild landscapes strewn with huge granite boulders, of forests and gorges, with many parts as unpopulated as they must have been in the Neolithic period that saw so many menhirs and dolmens erected in this magical area.

BELLE-ISLE-EN-TERRE (TO 02 96 43 01 71)

Belle-Isle really is an island - sort of - since the rivers Léguer and Guic circle round it. It is 'en terre' (on land) to distinguish it from the much better known Belle-Île, a real island off the south coast of Brittany. The château donated by a local girl who had married an Englishman and left Brittany (before eventually becoming Lady Mond, wife of the English industrialist), now houses the **Aquarium des Curieux de Nature** (02 96 43 08 39) and is open every afternoon in high summer for visitors to view a replica of river life from source to sea.

Explore the forest walks of Coat an Noz an Hay (the wood of night and day) on foot or by bike or horse, or join a group walk in the valley of the old paper mills leading to the disused dam at Kernansquillec, now a haven for wildlife. The 'sabotier' (clog maker) in the Place de l'Eglise invites visitors to view his work every Tuesday between 5 and 7 p.m. in July and August. (02 96 43 30 13)

Breton wrestling takes place on the third Sunday in July, and the blues Festival of the Two Rivers is in early October.

L'Abbaye de BON REPOS (02 96 24 82 20)

The Cistercian abbey here was originally founded in the 12th century by Alain III de Rohan, according to legend, after he had seen a vision of the Virgin in a dream whilst resting at this spot. It was initially populated by monks from Savigny in Normandy.

Abbaye de Bon Repos ©RDB

After the union of France and Brittany it came under lay abbots. In the 18th century, it was abbot Philippe Alexandre de Montault Saint-Genies Navaille who carried out renovations to the buildings, including the facade, which reflects his own luxurious tastes rather than those of the Cistercian monks. It was declared national property at the Revolution and sold to the mayor of Rostrenen. The Chouans partially burned it in 1795. In the 1830s it served as accommodation for the engineers building the Nantes-Brest Canal, after which it suffered from being used as a convenient source of building stone. It was rescued in the latter half of last century and is slowly being restored by the Association des Compagnons de l'Abbaye de Bon Repos.

The best approach to the Abbey is on foot from Perret or Gouarec and through the woods. Then, you can stop for a pot of Earl Grey tea in the charming Café de l'Abbaye whilst getting a good view of the façade.

The son et lumière evenings attract thousands and race haphazardly through bits of Breton history from grunting cave-men to oppressed prisoners building the canal. Children love it, but a word of advice: if you have sleepy young children, leave early to avoid the throng milling at snail's pace the half mile to the car park at midnight.

Drive north from the abbey through the Gorges du Daoulas.

BOURBRIAC (TO 02 96 43 46 03)

The church of St-Briac, with its remarkable Gothic porch, sits modestly at the base of the central square. The **ancient crypt** inside is well worth seeing. This dates from the 11th or 12th century and once contained the tomb of the saint. It now houses the early 16th century chapel of the Lords of Kerias dedicated to St-Lawrence.

Crypt ©RDB

The annual Festival de danse Plinn takes place during the first half of August with music and dance for all the family, and an enormous vide-grenier, sale of second-hand goods, is held in the same month at the sports stadium just outside the town. The library occasionally holds exhibitions, a memorable one of Celtic objects found nearby, although the local menhir and the Chaire des Druides, surrounded by maize fields and brambles, are over-rated. The Bronze Age Tumulus de Tanouédou is also in the vicinity. There are two shortish marked walks in the Koad Liou woods and the Plan d'Eau des Forges has a children's play area. Nearby at Plesidy, the Studi ha Studi gives courses and exhibitions in the Breton language and culture.

BULAT-PESTIVIEN (see also Pestivien)

Though no more than a 'bourg', Bulat-Pestivien warrants a visit on account of its church, a pilgrimage site since the fourteenth century. Its patron saint is St-Anne, the virgin mother of the Virgin Mary and the patron saint of grandmothers. The 'feunteun' (fontaine) in the churchyard enhances the milk of nursing mothers. A treacherous-looking spiral stone staircase leads to a viewing balcony on the steeple, the tallest in Côtes d'Armor. At the pardon on the second Sunday of September the villagers process behind a silver statue of Saint Anne and on the Monday the famous horse fair takes over the whole village. Book visits to the church and fountains on 02 96 45 70 21. Two other feunteuns are on the road to St-Anne (D50 direction Callac), one dedicated to the seven saints of Brittany.

©RDB

Charles de Blois, a medieval soldier/saint honoured here **(see page 28)**

©RDB

Church porch

Opposite the church, the 'maison du granit' houses a little exhibition and hosts talks and visits in the summer.

CALLAC (TO 02 96 45 90 29)

Callac has a dilapidated Roman bridge, which even some locals don't know is there, and the lovely ruined church of Botmel. It also has a statue of some consequence in the 1958 bronze of a Breton horse, the stud Naous, by the famous animal sculptor Georges Guyot, and it is a major centre for the breeding of Breton spaniels. Priding itself on its hunting tradition, Callac has managed to preserve some outstanding countryside even within the town itself. (See Walk No.4, page 93)

The Wednesday market has one of the best cheese stalls in Côtes d'Armor and another stall sells only pick'n'mix apples. Delicious! The Café de la Place is run by a friendly Welsh couple. The reservoir, le Lac de la Verte Vallée, has some pleasant walks and offers boating, fishing, mini-golf and tennis. For a different view of the Breton countryside, arrive at Callac by train from either Carhaix-Plouguer or Guingamp.

Naous ©RDB

◆CHATELAUDREN (TO 02 96 79 77 71)

Everywhere you go in Châtelaudren you come across bits of elegant architecture once belonging to what must have been a very beautiful château. This leads to some odd juxtapositions: wide stone steps sweep up terraces to arrive at a 1950s bungalow and, where you would expect to see a fine old building at the head of the lake, is, instead, a grain silo. But, nonetheless, this is a truly elegant town. The proportions of the central square are satisfying and the details - doorways, gable windows - on the houses are delightful.

In the refreshingly simple church a golden statue of God, very like a cherub, protects a couple of bleeding hearts and a golden St-Anne teaches her golden daughter, the Virgin Mary, to read.

©RDB

The large painted sign for the museum, **le Petit Echo de la Mode**, is a reminder of this hugely successful fashion magazine, which was founded in the late 19th century and led to a large publishing empire which brought its base to Châtelaudren in the 1920s. It took over the buildings of an old paper mill which had utilised turbines fed by the lake. Today the museum presents the history of le Petit Echo de la Mode and other exhibitions on themes such as printing.

The Rue des Moulins leads you past the Leff gushing from its dam to the lake where mechanical features of the mill can still be seen as well as a sailing school. A pleasant walk around the lake leads past tame cormorants by the picnic table and a children's play area.

The chapel on the hill, **Notre-Dame-du-Tertre**, looks uninviting with its huge sheets of modern stained glass but its red 15th century ceiling paintings in the choir and south chapel are justifiably famous. The 132 painted panels depict scenes from the Bible and legends of saints such as St-Fiacre and his miracles. It is open every day with guided visits in high summer. The pardon takes place on August 15th.

Le CHEMIN du PETIT TRAIN

The old metre-gauge railway track, part of the Réseau Breton (Breton Network) has been turned into a long-distance path which can be undertaken by foot or bike. It runs all the way from St-Meen Le Grand (35) to Carhaix-Plouguer (29), occasionally interrupted by later developments, but mostly intact, and in parts bordered by high banks and trees. Railway buffs will want to know of the book in English, *Reseau Breton* by Gordon Gravett published by The Oakwood Press (ISBN 0853615365).

COAT MAEL

Opposite the little chapel a track signposted to the **Pierres de Pempoul** leads to a path along the top of a field which leads in turn to an astonishing sight: six massive boulders, set boldly on top of each other in two groups of three.

There are so many boulders in this area it is hard to know what is natural formation and what has been deliberately set in place. These are said to be 'Celtic'.

Pierres de Pempoul ©PA

CORLAY (TO 02 96 29 42 90)

Before the advent of the car, Corlay must have been a confident market centre and it still retains some of that atmosphere though the castle and lake are now separated from the town by a major road and the church square is a car park. Corlay still appears to be obsessed by horses, boasting not only a hippodrome, the Petit Paris horse racing course on the Guingamp road, but also a **Musée du Cheval**, Museum of the Horse, at the castle.

For a change from horses, visit the angora goats at 'Mohair du Pays' on the way to Quintin, which is open every afternoon in summer except Sundays, and where the shaggy wool is transformed into skeins of fabulous colours and knitted items, which can be purchased.

GLOMEL

The lightness that Glomel seems to give out is perhaps due to the fact that it is not, like so many Breton villages, overshadowed by its church and, on the Nantes-Brest canal, it opens out into attractive countryside. Glomel has a nautical centre (02 96 29 65 01), a pleasant bar, a shop selling Marmite to ex-pats and some nice walks.

©RDB

Nantes-Brest Canal near Glomel

GORGES de TOUL-GOULIC

Just a few kilometres south-west of Lanrivain, off the D8 to Plounévez-Quintin, is the **Chaos of Toul-Goulic**, a deep rocky gorge, now a veritable sanctuary of natural beauty. It is a great place for children to leap over the boulders where the Blavet flows beneath.

GRACES

Just west of Guingamp, Grâces has a Sunday morning flea market, an unusual church and a rose nursery. The church here, in addition to rich architectural detail (including some amusing carvings), is best known for housing the reliquary of Charles de Blois who led the fight against the English-backed Montforts for succession to the dukedom of Brittany in the 14th century. He was defeated at the Battle of Auray in 1364, but the family of his widow, Jeanne de Penthièvre, carefully fostered the development of his cult and Charles was finally made a saint.

GUINGAMP (TO 02 96 43 73 89)

It is thought that Guingamp gave its name to the gingham it used to produce. An ancient ducal seat fortified against Viking invasions, it still retains a sense of its own importance, though the medieval buildings in the main square have been defaced by ugly shop-fronts, some even with flourescent lighting, and most of the tree-lined square is now a car park. But the attractive **Fontaine de la Plomée** and the little Saturday market can still be enjoyed from the tables outside the Grand Café while, inside, you can stand on a glass slab and look into the crypt below. The Hotel du Roy, also in the square, allows visitors into its courtyard to admire the ancient doorway.

Fontaine de la Plomée ©RDB

The porch of Notre-Dame de Bon Secours (next to the shop selling irrestible home-made nougat) is always alight with candles to the Black Virgin, dressed in starched white lace like any good Breton lady. The candle-lit procession of the pardon is held on the Saturday night before the first Sunday in July.

Follow the signs 'Circuit Médiéval', for an interesting walk round the town - the archaeological dig of the castle at the top of town is revealing layers of history and opposite it the huge car park is home to the bustling Friday market. Check your e-mails in the Internet Café at the bottom of the main square, or for the more adventurous, hire kayaks and canoe down the Trieux to Pontrieux.

Friday market ©RDB

During the third week in August, the town is taken over by a festival of Breton dance, and processions throng the streets bedecked with flowers.

KERGRIST MOËLOU

Church door at Kergrist ©RDB

Just north of Rostrenen, Kergrist is a gloomy place with a massive 16th century octagonal calvary and ancient yews in the churchyard central to the village. Eight American airmen are buried in the graveyard, their plane having been shot down in the war.

♦LANISCAT

The beautiful church in Laniscat is dedicated to St-Gildas, who is also the saint of the chapel in the nearby village bearing his name. It is one of the very few churches to have a bell wheel, turned 'to celebrate happy events', which, with its twelve bars and twenty four bells, is thought to have an association with the sun. The pardon is held on the last Sunday in January.

The saint, who helped cure and protect against rabies, is depicted on the nearby fountain with a dog and a cat, and a painting in the church bears witness to him having resuscitated a drowned child.

LANRIVAIN

Ossuary ©RDB

Though only a village, Lanrivain takes up a lot of space, its wide street opening into a large square with its church and generous graveyard where the 15th century ossuary is one of the few still to contain bones, and the calvary shows the thieves on their crosses. There is a cosy and outrageously friendly bar next to the excellent boulangerie le Roy, and a good-value restaurant, Chez Jerome et Virginie.

'Balades en caleche', excursions in horse-drawn carts, set out some evenings in summer. (02 96 45 76 31)

Allées couvertes de LISCUIS

Take the D44 southwards out of Laniscat and a right fork to follow the road up the hill to park at the base of a calvary missing its cross. Then walk up the high-banked track to the covered alley-grave, a burial tomb dating from the 4th to 2nd millenium BC, archaeologically ransacked for its contents but with its slate exterior still intact. From up here on the ridge, well-signed walks lead off temptingly in every direction and there are two more allées couvertes to discover. The site can be approached by foot from the D44 by climbing straight up the steep hill on the footpath below and opposite the well-situated camp site.

©RDB

Allée couverte, Lisuis

LOCARN

(TO 02 96 36 66 11)

Situated in steep hilly countryside, much of it wooded, Locarn reminds you that Côtes d'Armor is high on its granite mountain. The moors of the Landes de Locarn are an excellent walking area with marked paths leading from the car park at Quélénec (on the D20 toward St-Nicodème), which is dominated by a gigantic menhir. Cross the road and walk from here to the ♦**Gorges du Corong**, though this is not the only entrance. Though very popular and very old, the Gorges remain as fresh as Cleopatra and custom does not stale their infinite variety. At the bottom of the Gorges you can cross via the old oak which acts as a bridge and follow the track to a little chapel.

Around LOGUIVY-PLOUGRAS

There is something dignified about this sombre little town which, like so many others in the area, still retains painful memories from the two world wars. The countryside around it, hilly and in parts forested, is worth exploring and it includes the wonderful **Forêt de Beffou**. This well-preserved forest is laid out with paths and yet it is still possible to get well and truly lost. The huge granite outcrops typical of Brittany, hidden among the deciduous trees, are covered in lichen and moss. A delightful place to walk in all seasons.

MENEZ BRE

Though the Menez Hoguene and Menez Kerespers are actually higher than the bare, lonely Menez Bré, it is the Bré, last 'mont' in the chain of the Monts d'Arrée, that has captured the imagination of visitors and pilgrims alike. From here, views extend north beyond the valleys

©RDB

Chapel of St-Hervé

of the Jaudy, the Léguer and the Trieux to the sea, south towards Cornouaille and southwest to the Monts d'Arrée.

The chapel at the top is dedicated to the blind St-Hervé (always shown accompanied by his guide-wolf) who was both healer and exorcist. He is said to have created the spring on the hill. The chapel is open on Sunday afternoons in summer. This spot is also the legendary scene of the excommunication of Conomor, a 6th century ruler, whose many dastardly deeds, in legend, included the murder of his young wife and son, and one tradition makes him the Breton Bluebeard.

A ten kilometre walk around the Menez starts at the sports ground at Treglamus. The 'Grande Fête' of Breton horses takes place in mid-August.

MUR-de-BRETAGE

The 15th century (and later) chapel of Ste-Suzanne at the top of town, surrounded by oaks and yews, has more atmosphere than the main church and was often painted by Corot. Its ceiling is covered in 18th century paintings.

Mur acts as a staging post at the cross-roads linking east and west Brittany and the long straight road from the north which descends through the town and on to the fertile land of the south.

It is also the starting-off point for tourist trips to Lac de Guerlédan.

Chapel of Ste-Suzanne ©RDB

PESTIVIEN

Although Bulat-Pestivien is built on a site that goes back to the Bronze Age, the little hamlet of Pestivien precedes Bulat as a centre in Christian times.

The church of Pestivien is cold, uncomfortable and dilapidated but still wonderfully atmospheric in its simplicity. The keys can be obtained from the stonemason in the Presbytère, which houses a permanent art exhibition. The calvary in the churchyard depicts St-Nicodème and Joseph of Arimathea embalming the body of Christ. The stonemason gives an exuberant description.

PLOUISY

Perched above Guingamp to the northwest, Plouisy gives excellent views of the town and, since it is also situated on the long-distance GR footpath which runs along the River Trieux, interesting walks can be devised leading in and out of Guingamp.

But Plouisy is also worth a visit in itself, having its own château and 'Champ du Tir', a shooting range established by Napoleon III but now a pleasant place to walk.

PLUSSULIEN

Neolithic quarry ©RDB

Axe heads known to have been produced at Quelfenec over a period of almost two thousand years from 4,500 BC have been found at far-flung corners of Europe, making this a major **Neolithic site**. But you may find the educational notice board more illuminating than what is left of the quarry. The site is well-signed out of Plussulien and requires a short walk through woods. There are footpaths leading from the site for walks in the pleasantly rolling countryside.

♦QUINTIN (TO 02 96 74 01 51)

This town was on an important crossroads in Roman times, and its later economic history revolved around the weaving and textile industry. In 1789 there were more than 300 'tisserands' here. Today you can visit the **Maison des Tisserands**.

Notre-Dame ©PA

For a healthy stay, choose the Hippocamp (02 96 74 87 00) or the Hotel de la Vallée near the phallic war memorial at the bottom of town or, better still, the camp site. Jog round the lake in the park opposite and exercise on the 'parcours energie' before breakfast. Then pop into the public pool and sports centre at the camp site, stroll up to the menhir and have a round of 'swing golf'.

You should then be fit to climb the horrendously steep steps or path into the fortified town – if not, just amble up the road - to visit the **château** and the church of Notre-Dame (the pardon is the second Sunday in May), then to wander through the little streets and parks.

The Jardin des Carmes Fontaines, once owned by nuns, with its pruned trees around statuesque 'feunteuns' and surrounded by high, mellow stone walls is a calm retreat. In the cobbled square leading to it, the wisteria does honour to the old house fronts.

Market day is Tuesday but the Carrée aux Vaches beneath the city wall is no longer a cattle market. A stone-slabbed bridge, where the Gouet torrents over rocks and provides water for the lavoirs, leads out of the square but, going instead along the road next to the Bar le Dauphin, come to the Porte Neuf with ivy-clad round towers. And to find the marked walks, 'Sentiers de la Perche', go down the Rue de la Madeleine and on to the Chemin de la Perche.

ROSTRENEN (TO 02 96 29 02 72)

Rostrenen cannot be said to be a pretty town but it is interesting nonetheless. At the centre of an area rich in ecological enterprises and alternative life-styles, the Tuesday market attracts all sorts: stalls sell mohair, home-made shoes, second hand clothes, lemon yogurt, goat cheese, plants and wholemeal bread as well as the usual produce. The Bar le Bienvenu near the tourist office in the square is the rendezvous for local artists and opposite, you can check your e-mails.

Rostrenen centre ©RDB

Mid-August sees the 'Grand Pardon' of Notre Dame with a candle-lit procession, and towards the end of August, the three-day Festival Fisel, an energetic form of the rather sedate Breton dance, attracts thousands to the Hippodrome de Quenropers, and the atmosphere is electric.

Rando Rostren leads local walks. (02 96 29 03 37)

ROSQUELFEN

One of the most charming churches in the area (with an old Post Office letter-box on its wall) is perched up high in Rosquelfen, a village that until recently must have been all but inaccessible. The unusual 16th century calvary in the graveyard was damaged in the Revolution but the lichen covering adds to its beauty. The curate, too, was damaged by the Revolution – for refusing to swear allegiance to the civil constitution of the clergy, he was arrested from

©PA

his hide-out at Ste-Tréphine and sentenced to hard labour in French Guyana where he died a year later. The church's pardon is the first Sunday in July.

ST-FIACRE

The original saint of the church was the Irish St-Briac, who founded a hermitage in the forest of Lehart nearby. No-one knows why it was taken over by the equally Irish St-Fiacre in the sixteenth century. The 15th century south porch remains and a slightly later ossuary with eight 'boites à chef' or boxes to contain skulls. The bronze age Tumulus de Motten Hudolo is nearby, and a sculpture park.

ST-GUEN

St-Guen is a good mixture of the new and the old. The new lake offers a lot more than just a stopping point for passing cars. There is a pleasant walk, picnic areas and well-spaced children's games.

The church of St-Marie-Madeleine is exquisite with its rounded porch and square tower - be sure to view it, too, from the north end. The lavoir is both shrine and fontaine, as if to invoke the old alchemical motto: 'Do as the washerwoman does'.

ST-NICOLAS-du-PELEM (TO 02 96 29 52 51)

In the centre there is a charming fontaine and lavoir just below the church.

Fontaine ©RDB

The little camp site with its open-air swimming pool is placed near the river with excellent walks and behind the town the steep hills are covered in dense forest rising to moorland. A yellow-marked walk runs along the river Faoudel in the woods on the road to Lanrivain. A bit further north are the massive natural stones of Menez Plat.

The **School of Bothoa** (D5 north of St-Nicolas - 02 96 29 73 95), which closed down in 1977, has been reconstructed as a rural museum of education, giving visitors a chance to taste school life as it was in the 1930s when the school first opened.

The local walking group, les Marcheurs du Pelem, invites participants to join them on rambles. Contact the tourist office, which also arranges very popular night-time walks, sometimes with stories of the stars.

ST-THELO

St-Thélo, on the Route du Lin, demonstrates 'the story of flax' in its **Maison des Toiles** (02 96 56 38 26), an 18th century house once owned by a cloth merchant. The museum also organises day and night walks, trips in horse-drawn carriages and other events throughout the year. It is open every day in summer and at other times off season.

St-Thélo himself planted apple trees way up above the village at what is now Saints-Anges where the chapel, next to a bank of coloured quartz and known as the 'Door to the Forest', is dedicated to the angels from whom people would ask protection before crossing the forest. You can see the angel-heads on the stained glass windows from outside but to see the wooden statues of angels inside you need to get the key: information on the door.

STE-TREPHINE

The white-steepled church of Ste-Tréphine seeps peace and, although it is usually, like nearly all Breton churches, locked, you can sit in the sunny porch and admire the traces of delicate paintwork that still cling to the stone. To cure children suffering from bone deficiencies, people used to put them into the stone trough outside the oratory near the gate. At the other end of the oratory is a fluted menhir.

Beyond Ste-Tréphine is the hamlet of Trozulon where a picturesque chapel is falling into disrepair on the bank of the river Sulon.

Chapel at Trozulon

Le Chêne de TRONJOLY

This oak, fifteen hundred years old and once inhabited by a hermit, is situated in the courtyard of a friendly couple who welcome visitors any day except Sunday. To walk to it, take the GR from Pestivien to Kerluff then Cos Caraes and in the lower village follow the path behind the group of houses. To drive, turn right off the road from Bulat-Pestivien towards Guingamp.

COMMENTS

The wild moorland north of Kergrist-Moëlou and the forest to the east are a challenge to explore. For something completely different, Rostrenen market is lively and authentic, especially in summer.

From the charming Café de l'Abbaye you can get a view of the façade of Bon Repos whilst avoiding the commercial pressure to aid in the abbey's restoration. When you do cough up and see the work that has been done, you may not be so pleased you did. What is left of the abbey is certainly impressive, although the façade is totally at odds with the original building, but the more recently renovated part looks depressingly like any civic building.

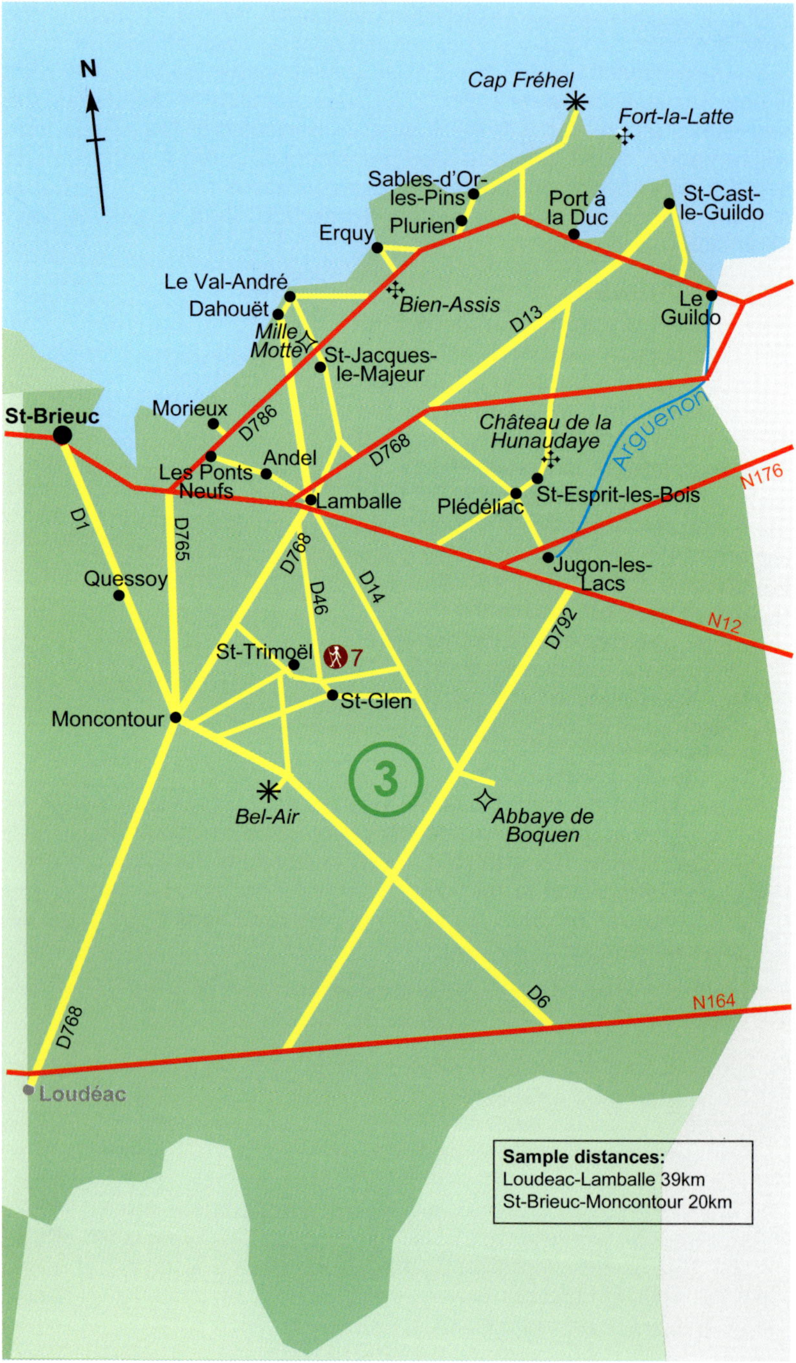
N
Cap Fréhel
Fort-la-Latte
Sables-d'Or-les-Pins
Plurien
Port à la Duc
St-Cast-le-Guildo
Erquy
Le Val-André
Dahouët
Bien-Assis
D13
Le Guildo
Mille Motte
St-Jacques-le-Majeur
Morieux
St-Brieuc
D786
Château de la Hunaudaye
Arguenon
D768
Andel
Les Ponts Neufs
Lamballe
Plédéliac
St-Esprit-les-Bois
N176
D1
D765
D768
D46
D14
Quessoy
Jugon-les-Lacs
N12
D792
St-Trimoël
7
St-Glen
Moncontour
3
Bel-Air
Abbaye de Boquen
D6
N164
D768
Loudéac
Sample distances:
Loudeac-Lamballe 39km
St-Brieuc-Moncontour 20km

3. Armor and Argoat, St-Brieuc eastwards

The Côte de Penthièvre, from St-Brieuc to Cap Fréhel, provides a whole series of enticing beaches and traditional holiday towns, such as Le Val-André and Erquy.

Historical interest abounds in the interior with the ancient centres like Lamballe, Moncontour and the Château de la Hunaudaye. The river Arguenon and forests dotted around also offer good walking and recreational activities in this varied region.

ANDEL

The little church at Andel is exquisite. Perfectly proportioned, it commands your attention not, like so many, by its domination but by its beauty and balance. Inside, the church is filled with light, the pale blue of the vaulted ceiling and the white and gold of the altar piece giving an effect of other-worldliness. Even the wooden statue and the stained glass window of St-Sebastian undergoing his torment do not disturb so much as soothe.

©RDB

Andel church

The presbytère next door is another perfectly proportioned building and its gable windows support little pottery animals overlooking the church. Another interesting house, this one with a tower, is on the road to St-Aaron.

BEL-AIR

The highest point in Côtes d'Armor and part of the chain of hills known as the Mene, Bel-Air was in Celtic times the centre of the cult of Belenos, the Sun god.

To walk there, start at the foot of the ruined château in Moncontour and follow the yellow and red signs out of the car park up Rue St-Michel. From the top the view stretches over the Forêt de Loudea, the Bay of St-Brieuc and the moors of the Mene. The Mene, or Landes du Menez, acted as the frontier between the counties of Penthièvre and Porhoët. It is also the site of sources which run northward towards the Channel and south to the Atlantic.

Bien-Assis ©PA

BIEN-ASSIS

Built in the 15th century, Bien-assis is a fairy-tale castle of pink stone with Rapunzel towers rising as from nowhere and surrounded not by one moat but two. But not much remains of the original castle except the massive tower at the back, and the château is a hotch-potch, some of it added in the 1620s and some not until the late 18th century. During the Revolution the château was taken over and, after having been used as a prison, came under the ownership of one of Napoleon's generals. It was bought by the Kerjegus family in the late 19th century.

The grounds with their long avenues of oak and beech retain their sense of both history and mystery. Open from Easter to 1st October Sundays and public holidays 2-6.30; from mid-June to mid-September daily 10.30-12.30 and 2-6 (except Sunday morning).

Abbaye de BOQUEN

Hidden away in the Forest of Boquen, the abbey, founded by the Cisterican order in 1137 with monks and an abbot from Bégard, became a ruin after the Revolution and was only brought back to life by Mathurin Presse, alias Dom Alexis Presse, who from 1936 organised the necessary help and funds to re-establish monastic life at the abbey. Since the 1970s it has been occupied by the Sisters of Bethlehem who give guided tours.

DAHOUET and SENTIERS DES DOUANIERS

The footpath used by customs officers runs all along the coast and in some places the guardhouses still exist. The one that still stands at Port de Dahouët was built in 1750 to keep watch over the bay and this stretch of coast.

At the port of Dahouët, Newfoundland fishing boats were built. Walks are sometimes organised to visit the port, the shipbuilders' houses and the maritime history workshop. (02 96 72 20 55)

From the port of Dahouët boats leave for the Isle of Bréhat.

ERQUY (TO 02 96 72 30 12)

A pleasant stroll at Erquy, famous for its scallops, leads along the promenade to the complex of little fish restaurants and beyond them to the fenced-off Port de Pêche. From here, the view of the sea is spectacular but the town itself with its routine architecture lacks the intimacy and originality of similar ports elsewhere.

The pink stone church of Saints Peter and Paul, with its well-worn steps, in the Place du Centre, is divided inside into three aisles by Romanesque arches and, when your eyes have adjusted to the gloom, you gradually appreciate the contrasting brightness of the stained glass - St-Michael slaying the dragon on the round window at the back - and the cool, calm spaciousness of the building with its high vaulted ceiling. The Romanesque chancel was rebuilt in the 15th century by the Lords of Bien-Assis, and the east gable and Gothic window were erected around 1414 by Geffroy du Quelenec. A prayer on the wall suggests that taking the time to reflect is the source of power and reading is the base of wisdom.

The chapel on the hill, Notre-Dame-des-Croix-Sept-Saints, with its 14th century wooden statue of the Virgin, was a pilgrimage site and a resting place on the route between Mont St-Michel and St-Jacques de Compostelle. It is also known as la Chapelle des Marins and sailors used to pray here before setting out on long sea journeys. While the church of Sts-Pierre and Paul honour the dead from the two world wars, this little chapel records the names of drowned sea-men.

The ransacked chapel of St-Michel on the little island of Rochecoul is about to undergo restoration.

◆FORT-la-LATTE (02 96 41 40 31)

If you can manage to approach Fort-la-Latte on foot by the old Sentier des Douaniers which goes right by it, you could appreciate what really is a stunning apparition and one that gives a true sense of history since the castle, built in the 13th and 14th centuries, is pretty much still intact. There are many points on the road where you can leave your car and take to the heath to join the footpath on the edge of the cliff.

The castle is, in fact, quite low so the view as you arrive is from above but this has not weakened its impregnability. From its small rocky island

On the cliff path near Fort-la-Latte ©PA

separated from the mainland by two gorges over which visitors cross by draw-bridge, it commands a spectacular view of the bay and beyond and, while acting as a stronghold, it also retains the air of an enclosed village. The atmosphere is greatly aided by the family who bought the castle in 1931 thereby, unwittingly, saving it from becoming, like so many others, a civic enterprise. It has often been used as a film-set, and a visit today includes former living quarters, the chapel and the keep as well as the outer fortifications.

Even today, if you arrive in winter, you see smoke coming from the chimneys and can almost hear the crow of the cocks and the sound of the church bells. From the top of the tower perched above the sea you feel the exhilaration of being on top of the world and can see up the Emerald Coast to the Cherbourg peninsula and right out to the Channel Islands.

Open June-September and Easter holidays 10-12.30 and 2.30-6.30 and the rest of the year on weekends and public holidays 2.30-5.30.

Cap FREHEL

If you come to Brittany to get away from it all, then Cap Fréhel is not for you. To get a view of the sea visit the 'panoramic' restaurant and lighthouse or to get a glimpse of the birds in the reserve, you may have to jostle a few of your fellow visitors off the cliffs.

©RDB

Better by far to stop at one of the many other glorious view points along the cliffs, easily accessible from the road. Or, if you do go to Cap Fréhel, treat it as a starting point to walk to Fort-la-Latte along the Sentier des Douaniers - which should take about an hour and forty minutes.

Le GUILDO

The beach at Quatre-Vaux is more rural than that at St-Cast. Walks on the Sentier Touristique take you through the smart holiday resort around the beach of Pen Guen and the Pointe de la Garde. The long-distance GR footpath winds through wooded lanes towards the Arguenon: its wide muddy estuary is a haven for bird-life and pairs of egrets can be spotted near the bridge.

Park in the car park here on the west bank, visit the little Galerie Pierres Sonnantes (which can be rented for holidays: 02 96 41 18 80) and walk up the path beside the river to come to **les Pierres Sonnantes** (Singing Stones). Now clearly marked with a 'PS', they lie in formation having been thrown up many aeons ago by the giant Gargantua who had eaten them for dinner having, to judge by their clean-cut edges, first neatly carved them. You are supposed to be able to get a ringing sound if you hit the stones with a piece of the amphibol of which they are made.

The view of the ruined castle of le Guildo just over the river, especially at dawn and dusk, evokes a long-gone era when the Arguenon formed the frontier between the lordships of Dinan and Penthièvre. If you cross the bridge to the atmospheric Port du Guildo you can walk around the 14th century castle. A track leading off to the right from the main road heading towards Plancoët leads to a neolithic 'allée couverte'.

♦La HUNAUDAYE

The castle at La Hunaudaye, dating from 1220 and at one time the most strategically important and powerful in the whole area, controlling the frontier between Penthièvre and Poudouvre, is what castles should be: fortified with five round towers and strong curtain walls and surrounded by a moat. Its history lives up to its promise too. Built and owned by the Tournemire family, it was destroyed following Brittany's War of Succession. Reconstructed in the 15th century, and made more comfortable in the 17th century, it was then set on fire during the Revolution in the 18th.

Visitors can watch a video about the underground passages and on Wednesday evenings in season, attend 'spectacles' including theatre, outdoor cinema and fire-eating. Nearby, there are laid-out walks in the woods of La Hunaudaye.

It is open every day between mid-June and mid-September and on Sundays and bank holidays from April 1st to November 1st. To book a guided visit: 02 96 34 82 10.

©RDB

JUGON-LES-LACS (TO 02 96 31 70 75)
Originally the site of a château, the history of this town revolves around water. It was Pierre de Dreux, Duke of Brittany in the 13th century, who saw the defensive potential of flooding the river valleys, since when the inhabitants have become adept at managing water. The castle was dismantled under Richelieu's orders in the early 17th century but the town and its lakes remained and today are a centre for all kinds of watery leisure pursuits from fishing to just walking by the lakes.

♦**LAMBALLE** (TO 02 96 31 05 38)
Despite the major roads and industrial estates that surround it, Lamballe remains one of the most appealing towns in Côtes d'Armor, the rounded church spire of St-John rising from the mound on which the old part of the city is built.

Maison du Bourreau ©RDB

The capital of the duchy of Penthièvre between 1134 and 1420, the town dates from the eleventh century and retains its air of antiquity with cobbled streets leading off the main square (given over to market on Thursdays), precariously leaning medieval houses with little terracotta statues on some of the roofs and old stone bridges over the Gouessant and its tributaries, which lead easily into pleasant countryside walks.

To the side of the Place du Champ de Foire, which holds a small Sunday market, is the **Haras**, where the public can watch the horses of the National Guard put through their paces every day in summer at 10.30 and 5.30 and at other times off season (02 96 50 06 98). Beyond it is the attractive church of St-Martin with its ornate porch.

Le Musée d'Art Populaire, located with the Tourist Office and the museum of the artist, Mathurin Mehuet, in the 15th century **Maison du Bourreau** (House of the Executioner), retraces the history of Lamballe and displays a model of the town in 1420 before the destruction of the château and ramparts. The cultural centre, Quai des Rêves, has a lively programme of music, dance and theatre. At the end of September, horse demonstrations and spectacles take place in the Parc Equestre beyond the haras.

Haras ©RDB

♦MONCONTOUR (TO 02 96 73 49 57)

Montcontour, at one time a major site defending the duchy of Penthièvre including its capital Lamballe, is so well fortified behind heavy walls on its isolated hill that it is easy to drive straight past it. But mounting the steep streets into the town, stopping to take in the views both within the town and beyond it, you soon feel you have entered another era and on a summer's day, the lazy feel of siesta behind the doors of the elegant houses built with wealth from the linen trade is reminiscent of the Mediterranean.

©PA

Much of the town was destroyed by Cardinal Richlieu, governor of Brittany in the early 1600s, yet the ancient walls still give a sense of history. The church of St-Mathurin, built in the 16th century and retaining six renaissance stained-glass windows generally considered to be the most beautiful in Brittany, is now the focus for the town. St-Mathurin was known for his ability to heal the mentally ill and the religious festival, or pardon, is held in his honour at Whitsun.

The **Museum of the Revolution** gives a true-to-life picture of the ever fascinating Revolution and the resistance to it, while the **Museum of Theatre Costumes** contents itself with portraying the events of history from the thirteenth to the twentieth century through costume from stage and films.

MORIEUX

It is not surprising that Morieux has renamed its main square with the date that the war came to an official end, 8 May 1945. Coastal towns and villages were not only invaded by the Germans but bombed and shelled by the British liberation forces. On the beach of St-Maurice, an extremely solid gun emplacement still stands while on the cliff above it, the little chapel, which was devastated during the war and then left open to the winds for forty years, has now been

©RDB

restored. To get to it, take the little road out of Morieux behind the boulangerie and then the left fork.

Swimming in the sea at St-Maurice can be dangerous because of the hydro-electric works behind it. At times the dam is opened letting the waters of the Gouessant rush into the sea. Though the cliffs are low at this point, the views along the sandy sweep of St-Brieuc bay are stunning and the GR footpath heads up river to Pont Rolland (45 mins) or along the cliffs to the view points, Jospinet (1h15) and La Cotentin (2h).

In the Romanesque village church, 12th century frescoes were recently discovered. Guided visits are available between April and November. (02 96 32 74 28)

Les PONTS-NEUFS

©RDB

The viaduct at les Ponts-Neufs once carried trains from St-Brieuc along the coastal route but, sadly, it is now only the main road that runs through the village. You can, though, get off the beaten track by taking the little road towards Andel, driving past the lake and over a little bridge. Then, if you turn right down the track which leads to a car park, you can watch the heron lift off on slow beating wing and take a (45 min) walk around the lake.

PORT à la DUC

It is more than a pity, a tragedy, that the little train no longer potters along its magnificent coastal route, and nowhere do you feel it more than at Port à la Duc where you can still see the viaduct running above the little road that leads between the sea wall and high rocks out to the Vieux Port. At low tide the enormous river estuary is a bird-watcher's dream, and it is not only the birds that are searching for shell-fish. If you look out to sea from the old stone jetty (where a memorial plaque honours fifteen young men who attempted to leave from here for England during the second World War), you might spot a tractor puffing over the sands to gather cockles and mussels. From here, you can walk to Fort-la-Latte (2h l5min) or Cap Fréhel (3h l5min) or take the shorter, yellow-signed river walks. The number 2 bus stops here from Pays de Fréhel and Sables-d'Or-les-Pins so walks could be devised to return by bus.

QUESSOY

The name 'Quessoy' means 'middle of the woods' or 'oak' so it is appropriate that the council have established an arboretum at nearby Carnivet where they have planted several hundred varieties of oak.

©RDB

Also nearby is the **allée couverte** of Champ Grosset. The information board in the village shows a 12 km footpath which passes it.

SABLES-d'OR-Les-PINS

The road leading to the beach is wide enough for a couple of football pitches and the houses, hotels and restaurants on either side recall the grandeur of the 1920s when Sables d'Or was invented as a tourist resort. But the crash of the 1930s brought disaster and the resort has never been finished, leaving a rather wild sense to the place as if it is battling against an inevitable return to the elements.

The beach of golden sand is one of the most accessible in the area but it manages to retain its peace and privacy. Pines all along the cliffs give a Mediterranean feel and here the GR footpath crosses the road and passes through moorland and woods.

Sables-d'Or-Les-Pins

©RDB

SAINT-ESPRIT-des-BOIS, PLEDELIAC

The little village of Saint-Esprit is home not only to the massive castle of La Hunaudaye (see page 41) but also to the **Ecomusée de la Ferme d'Antan**, a pretty little farm with a thatched bee on its thatched roof. The farm, which was bought in 1974 by the local 'Association of Past and Present', gives an account of how a peasant family would have lived at the turn of the 20th century. It is open from April to September from 2-6pm and in June, July and August from 10-6 every day except Sunday and Monday morning (02 96 34 80 77). Fifty yards up the road from the museum a large stone grinding wheel can be seen.

A sign-post outside the chapel points to a 3h walk in the Forest of La Hunaudaye and a large notice board on the corner of the museum gives information on other walks.

ST-BRIEUC (TO 02 96 33 32 50)

Badly damaged during the war, the centre of St-Brieuc, the 'city of valleys', now seems too small and compressed for its rambling hinterland which spreads inland to dramatic quarries and along the river to the run-down port and the sea.

The **Cathedral of St-Etienne** still stands, much restored after its ill-fortunes during the Revolution, when a great deal of the fine decorative detailing was destroyed during its spell as a stables. One quality Baroque altarpiece by Yves Corlay survives. Ancient houses remain in the picturesque streets to the north-west of the cathedral.

©RDB

Old house, now a restaurant

The nearby **museum** holds an interesting collection of Breton art, crafts and history (closed Sunday mornings and Monday), and the grand opera house in its square has survived.

Under the viaduct on the left bank of the river small restaurants serve fish meals, and the pottery, set back in a huddle of little streets, has an exhibition of local archaeological finds on the top floor of its perilous medieval building. Following the river round to the sea, there are coves with huge expanses of sand and mountains of scallop shells washed up against the cliffs.

ST-CAST (TO 02 96 41 81 52)

The local photographer takes his wedding groups to the dunes at St-Cast for romantic pictures of swirling white against the silvery sands.

©RDB

There are, in fact, seven good beaches at St-Cast but the one by St-Cast itself offers everything. From the Pointe de St-Cast on the cliff at one end of the beach, you can see Fort-la-Latte across the Bay of la Fresnaye and from the Pointe de la Garde at the other end, you can look over the beaches of St-Cast and Pen Guen and take walks along the cliff.

The huge expanse of sand is home not only to the usual water-sports but also to volley-ball, organised games for children and adults (Clubs de Plage) and explorations of the rock pools for kids (Centre Nautique) and, though at low tide the trek to the sea across swathes of flat sand might take a while, it is time well spent. Food and drink can be bought easily enough on the beach but it is a real treat to wander to the elegant cafés and sit in the pedestrianised square while the children ride the merry-go-round.

The church of Notre-Dame has a 16th century font and 17th century statues. A column nearby, on which a greyhound (France) defeats a leopard (England) commemorates a battle of 1758 in the Seven Years War. While they were returning from St-Malo to their warships anchored in the bay of St-Cast, 2,400 British soldiers, led by General Bligh, were killed or drowned when attacked by the troops of the Duke of Aiguillon, Governor of Brittany.

At l'Isle, the old fishing village now incorporated into the town, the chapel is, more peacefully, dedicated to St-Blanche, mother of St-Guénolé, St-Jacut and St-Venec.

ST-GLEN

The peaceful village of St-Glen, gathered round the attractive church of St-Etienne with its 18th century sundial, owes its name to a sixth century Irish monk, Sanctus Gallamus. Situated on the old Roman road and with the river Gouessant flowing through it and on to the reservoir at the Moulin Corbel, it offers some good walking. Park, for instance, on the road to Trédaniel and take the marked path up-river past the mill on the left. (Also, see Walk No.7, page 102). The moated feudal 'motte' at la Haie au Lion can be visited with the permission of the owner.

Church of St-Etienne

ST-JACQUES-le-MAJEUR

From the outside it looks as if the tower of the church has partly collapsed but in fact it was never finished. Dating from the l3th century or earlier, the church has a Templar connection and a number of local lords are known to have joined the Crusades. Situated on the road from St-Alban to St-Malo, St-Jacques used to receive pilgrims, accommodating them in wooden buildings that are known to have been standing in the grounds of the church in the 16th century.

Jean III, Duke of Brittany, built the western gable between 1312 and 1328 and the bell, cast in 1617 and named Maria, is the oldest in the department. On the side of the church, adjacent to the main road, a frieze adorning the arcades shows a beast being chased by dogs, a symbolic representation, it has been suggested, of justice chasing the thief, since by an edict of 1436 a judge came to the village annually on the eve of St-Jacques to pursue the cause of justice.

©PA

The church had the confidence to make its post-war repairs an opportunity for a further landmark in its fascinating history. The bare wooden ceiling and beams and plain walls give a simple, serious atmosphere which sets off the mural that runs round the walls like a wide dado rail. Commissioned in the 1950s, it depicts the stations of the cross in raised concrete interspersed with quotations from the Bible, painted, along with symbols and diagrams, to give the effect of hieroglyphs. The stained-glass window portraying the lives of St-Jaques and St-Alban dates, too, from the bold era of the `50s.

From St-Jacques, footpaths marked in red and green lead through the pleasant hilly countryside.

ST-TRIMOEL

The little parish church, originally Notre-Dame, then, for unexplained reasons, the Chapelle de Trève is one of the very few that leaves its door wide open and welcomes visitors with a written greeting just inside.

Opposite the grotesque crucifixion scene on its fake Golgotha just up the road from the church are a couple of wattle-and-daub cottages.

There are walks from St-Trimoël to the reservoir where you can walk along the river passing the old mills. (See Walk No.7, page 102)

©RDB

Le VAL-ANDRE (TO 02 96 63 00 24)

Perfect family holiday beaches, Le Val-André and the adjacent Plage des Vallées are long stretches of sand with endless natural amusement for children - exploring the rocks and pools, examining an impressive range of stones from black and deep purple through veiny pinks and blues to bright orange and white, collecting an assortment of shells and, of course, splashing in the sea. Little rocky islands attract bird life and sand pipers run along the edge of the water.

You can go by foot to Plage des Vallées down the path from Pléneuf centre that leads through a little tree-lined park along the river, stopping en route at the children's play area and, once at the sea, if you amble eastwards along the sands to Plage Nantois where a house stands in ruins on the golf course, you can walk back over the cliff. A little restaurant on the sea front at the car park supplies all your needs for the day.

The wider and still more popular Plage du Val-André has a nautical centre and sand-surfers race along the beach. The tourist office is situated in the centre next to the casino and play area. At the eastern end a footpath runs along the bottom of the cliff leading, at low tide, to the Île du Verdelet, a bird sanctuary known for its cormorants.

Guided rambles set out on Thursdays at 8 pm in July and August from the Plage des Vallées or the harbour at Dahouët. (02 96 63 02 18)

©RDB

Le Val-André

COMMENTS

St-Cast is a real, old-fashioned family resort and its near neighbour St-Guildo, with its crumbling château on the river and its 'Singing Stones' can finish off a perfect day. Away from the coast, treading the old stones in the towns of Lamballe and Montcontour evokes a timeless sense of peace.

The château at La Hunaudaye, with renovation work underway and the woods around cleared, is now in danger of becoming a bit too cleaned up. The castle, still awesomely mighty but having lost much of its imposing landscape, is beginning to look a bit tame.

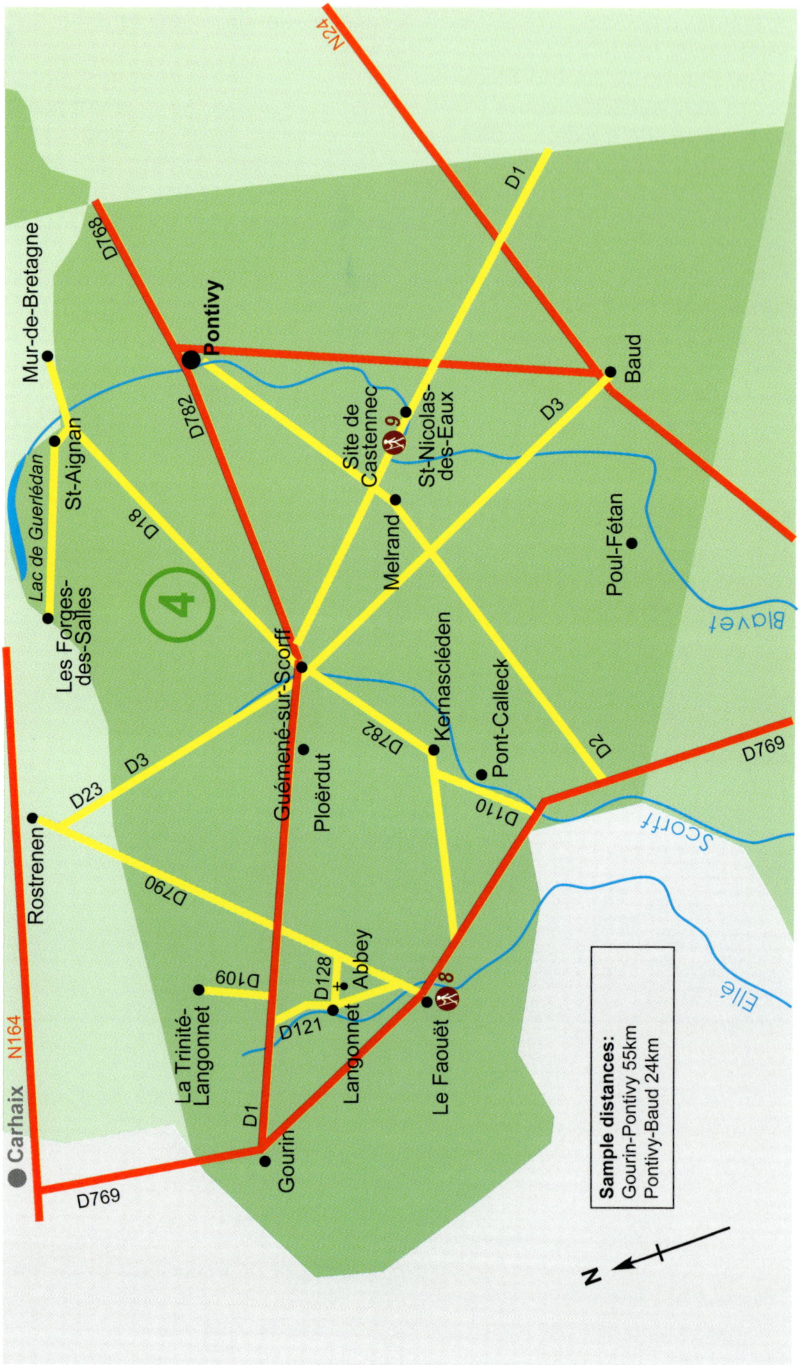

Mur-de-Bretagne
Pontivy
Baud
St-Aignan
Lac de Guerlédan
Les Forges-des-Salles
Site de Castennec
St-Nicolas-des-Eaux
Melrand
Poul-Fétan
Guémené-sur-Scorff
Kernascléden
Pont-Calleck
Ploërdut
Rostrenen
La Trinité-Langonnet
Langonnet
Abbey
Le Faouët
Gourin
Carhaix
N164
N24
D768
D782
D1
D3
D18
D2
D23
D790
D109
D128
D121
D110
D769
Blavet
Scorff
Ellé
4
8
9
Sample distances:
Gourin-Pontivy 55km
Pontivy-Baud 24km
N

4. The Argoat of Morbihan westwards from Pontivy

The hinterland of western Morbihan is bordered on the north by the eastern end of the Black Mountains and drained by beautiful rivers, the Ellé, the Scorff, the Blavet and their tributaries. The upper reaches of the Scorff are particularly attractive while the majestic Blavet has been canalised from its mouth at Lorient up to Pontivy, where it beomes an integral part of the Nantes-Brest Canal. The countryside is peppered with little chapels from the 16th/17th centuries and even earlier. Two outstanding examples can be visited at Le Faouët (see Walk No.8). There is also the historic town of Pontivy to explore.

BAUD

Sunday market ©RDB

The pleasant little town of Baud is the home of an extensive collection and exhibition of old Breton postcards, providing an exceptional record of custom, culture, festivals, costume and architecture since the 19th century. **Cartopole** can be found in what were once the public swimming baths, near the fire station.

Just outside Baud is a curiosity of decidedly non-traditional origins. In an interesting garden, once part of the Château de Quinipily (long since destroyed), stands a huge granite figure of a naked pagan goddess, the so-called **Venus of Quinipily**. Its appearance in this area may have something to do with the presence of Roman soldiers at nearby Castennec (Sulis), and it has been identified variously with the Egyptian goddess Isis and the Celtic/Asiatic mother deity Cybele. The statue was the focus of pagan rituals in the 17th century to the extent that the Bishop of Vannes demanded it be destroyed and Claude de Lannion, Lord of Quinipily, saw it was thrown into the Blavet in 1661. Fished out again by adherents of this 'Guardian' figure three years later, orders were given to destroy it once and for all, but after a few attempts at defacement, the statue found itself at the bottom of the river once more. In 1698, Pierre, son of Claude and now master of Quinipily, retrieved the Venus and, fighting off a legal challenge from the Duke of Rohan, took her into the grounds of his château, where she still stands today on her plinth above a fontaine.

©RDB

♦CASTENNEC, Site of

Castennec (Castel-Noec) was an important site in Roman times, under the name Sulis, situated on the main Carhaix to Vannes road. It became a feudal fortress in the territory of the ruling house of Porhoët whose seat was at Josselin. Alain, brother of Geoffroi, count of Porhoët, made Castennec his base before moving to Rohan at the beginning of the 12th century. There is little to see here today except the fabulous view from the belvedere, and a chapel with its neighbouring picnic area. A short walk (for directions see Walk No.9, page 108, paragraph 3) takes you to another chapel, that of St-Gildas, under an overhanging rock beside the Blavet.

Chapel of St-Gildas ©RDB

Le FAOUËT (TO 02 97 23 23 23)

A market town serving a rural area and noted for its fine 17th century timber and slate-roofed market hall. At the southwest corner of the market square a convent contains a **museum of local paintings** (open April-Sept). Just to the north of the town, the **Chapelle de Ste-Barbe** nestles under a cliff and is reached by an impressive baroque staircase. The chapel was built in the late 15th century by Jean de Toulbodou who, whilst hunting at this spot, was miraculously saved from falling rocks when lightning struck the cliff-face above him. The chapel contains some fine early 16th century stained glass. To the south of Le Faouët stands the **chapel of St-Fiacre**. The interior has been restored to show off its polychromed rood screen (jubé) as well as other items of religious carving in both wood and stone. (See Walk No.8, page 104)

Inside the roof of the market hall ©RDB

Les FORGES-des-SALLES

©RDB

This is an 18th/19th century ironworking village of about 30 buildings, grouped around its tall furnace. The village remains basically unchanged since industrial activity here ceased in 1880, some buildings have been restored to their original purpose, others as exhibition areas. The setting, in a valley of the Forêt de Quénécan not far from the Abbey of Bon Repos, is idyllic. However, its opening times are rather limited so your visit needs careful planning to avoid disappointment. Open from Easter to 1st November weekends and holidays from 2.00 to 6.30; July and August every day from 2.00 to 6.30. (02 96 24 90 12)

GOURIN (TO 02 97 23 66 33)

Gourin is unremarkable most of the year but on the third weekend in July it hosts a 'Festival of the Crêpe', a culinary delight for which the town is famous, with traditional music, dancing, a lot of crêpe eating, a fest-noz on Saturday night and a fest-deiz on Sunday afternoon. On the first weekend in September the town comes alive again for the Breton traditional music championships. These normally take place at the **Château de Tronjoly**, an elegant 18th century mansion on the northern outskirts of the town, acquired by the local commune in 1984 and since restored. It is open to the public in the sense that it is the setting for various exhibitions and events throughout the summer, but the grounds can be visited at any time.

GUEMENE-SUR-SCORFF (TO 02 97 39 33 47)

A pleasant little town that used to have a castle until 1920 when it was demolished, leaving only the **Rohan Gate** to be saved as a monument and an inconvenient obstruction to traffic! The town centre contains some late medieval houses (booklet available at TO), notably the 'Hotel des Princes', sadly neglected and with an ugly modern shop front but remarkable none the less. Local hero Hippolyte-Magloire Bisson is commemorated in street names. He was a French naval officer, serving in the Aegean in 1827, who died heroically while in command of a

Rohan gate

prize ship, choosing to blow up the ship and himself with it rather than surrender to Greek pirates. There is a full length portrait of him in the council chamber at the mairie. Otherwise, the town is traditionally famous for its *andouilles*, a type of pork sausage.

Hotel des Princes ©RDB

For some especially attractive countryside take the D3 north as far as Langoëlan. The road follows the Scorff towards its source and the hills and woods look incredibly green and peaceful.

♦KERNASCLEDEN

At **Kernascléden** to the southeast of Le Faouët the church, from the mid 15th century and connected to the famous Rohan family, contains some interesting early wall paintings including a 'dance of death' complete with torture scenes, and episodes from the lives of the Virgin and Christ. (See also page 16 for a similar fresco at Kermaria.)

©RDB

LAC de GUERLEDAN

The lake was created in 1928 with the construction of a barrage to generate hydro-electric power: it effectively cut in half the Nantes-Brest Canal. The lake, in fact an enormous reservoir, with its swimming beaches, cafés and watersports is very busy in high season. There are many walks in its 'forest' of plantation pines and rigid trackways, a contrast to the far more interesting Bois de Gouarec further west where you can walk the network of paths with only the deer, birds and elves for company.

©RDB

♦Abbaye de LANGONNET

Those in search of medieval buildings may be slightly disappointed on visiting the abbey of Langonnet. Although it was founded in 1136, all that remains from that period is the much restored Chapter House, now used as a chapel. The rest of this assemby of monumental buildings is comparatively recent but laden with atmosphere. To really appreciate it one perhaps needs to know something of its history, which is a sad reflection of the troubled history of Brittany over the centuries.

The abbey was established at Langonnet on lands granted by Conan III, Duke of Brittany, prompted by his mother the dowager duchess Ermengarde, who was an admirer of St-Bernard de Clairvaux, a leading light in the Cistercian order. The twelve monks who came from the Abbaye de l'Aulmone near Chartres, found that the remoteness of the spot, 'this land of granite covered with oaks' suited them well, although Conan had insisted on a percentage of the abbey's harvest in return for the land.

©RDB

Whilst Brittany was independent, the abbey became rich thanks to the piety and generosity of the peasants and local lords. When the Act of Union with France was signed in 1532, it came under the same 'Régime de Commende' as French abbeys, whereby the king could appoint a layman as abbot, a system whose abuse often led to the impoverishment of religious houses and the decay of their buildings. During the Wars of Religion (1590-1598) the abbey was taken over by a band of Ligueurs, ostensibly fighting for the Catholic cause but in fact a bunch of brigands under their notorious leader La Fontenelle, who evicted the monks, ransacked the abbey and turned the abbey church into a stable. The abbey was then fought over back and forth and when the monks finally returned they found nothing but ruins.

Between 1688 and 1788 the abbey was reconstructed, only to succumb to the French Revolution in 1790, when it became the property of the nation. The library was dispersed, the bells melted down, and the farm implements sold at auction. No buyer was forthcoming for the buildings and they were let to three tenants.

In 1793 the abbey became a rendez-vous for Chouans, the Catholic, anti-revolutionary resistance movement, and recalcitrant priests. It was consequently attacked and then garrisoned by the republicans. By 1803 it had become a shelter for all the hopeless poor people of the area, housing about sixty families in appalling conditions of squalor and lawlessness.

In 1806 the abbey was taken over by the National Haras and became a centre for breeding war horses. Then in 1856 the Congrégation du Saint-Esprit, who were looking for a home for their order, exchanged their convent in Hennebont for the abbey at Langonnet, which is why the National Haras is at Hennebont today.

The abbey is still in the possession of the Congrégation du Saint-Esprit and performs the functions of a retirement home for about forty missionaries, as well as a retreat for those seeking a period of reflection and prayer, and a missionary administration centre. It is the missionary aspect that has led to the **Museum of Africana**, which can also be visited.

Ploërdut ©RDB

PLOËRDUT

The church dates from the 13th century and is worth a look in passing. The interior is Romanesque and the charnel house on the south side of the tower is more enclosed than many examples to be seen in Brittany.

PONT-CALLECK

South of the D782 between Le Faouët and Kernascléden, the D110 leads to the Forest of Pont-Calleck. There used to be a château at Pont-Calleck, the property of the Marquis de Pontcallec, but it was largely destroyed in 1593 during the Wars of Religion. In 1718 the Marquis de Pontcallec was a prominent member of a conspiracy of minor Breton aristocracy that banded together to defend the terms of the treaty of 1532 (binding Brittany to France) and in opposition to the corrupt and overbearing French administration of Brittany by the ministers of the regent (this being the time of Louis XV's minority). This rebellion, poorly conceived and executed, soon fizzled out, but the Marquis de Pontcallec, who had taken refuge with the Curé of Lignol, was arrested and eventually executed in Nantes. The château at Pont-Calleck was rebuilt in the nineteenth century and is now a children's home (Notre-Dame-de-Joie). You can walk in the grounds and visit the lake, or, continuing further down the road, there are pleasant walks in the forest, and alongside the Scorff.

©RDB

♦PONTIVY (TO 02 97 5 04 10)

The town of Pontivy is situated on the Blavet river, part of the Nantes-Brest Canal here. In legend, it was founded by St Ivy who came from Lindisfarne in the 7th century AD. The 15th century Château de Rohan dominates the northern part of the town, in sharp contrast to the later Napoleonic development so much in evidence in the modern centre. It is a busy place with a large market on Tuesdays in the huge square originally designed for military reviews.

Pontivy rose to importance when it became the main seat of the Rohan family, who moved here from nearby Rohan after both castles were destroyed in the mid-14th century wars of succession. In 1485, the current **Château de Rohan** at Pontivy, a fine example of medieval architecture, was begun.

The Rohans were one of the few Protestant families of the Breton nobility, and a reform church was founded by Henri I de Rohan in Pontivy in 1561. The town was taken by the Catholic army, including Spanish troops, in 1589 during the Wars of Religion, but returned to the Rohans after the Edict of Nantes, proclaiming tolerance, in 1598.

The town suffered something of a decline in the 18th century, and it eagerly embraced the ideals of the French Revolution. Although the anti-revolutionary Chouan movement, which supported the Catholic church and restoration of the French monarchy, was strong in the region of Morbihan, Pontivy remained a staunchly republican town. Its reward was to be chosen by Napoleon as a suitable military centre for keeping law and order in the surrounding countryside. It would also provide a vital link in the chain of the new canal planned from Nantes to Brest.

The town was renamed Napoleonville in 1804 and a new lay-out of the centre was conceived. The Place Aristide Briand gives a good idea of the scale of this development, and buildings around it such as the Hotel

Napoleonville, the early 19th century development of Pontivy ©RDB

de Ville retain their period facades. Just across the river is the former barracks building.

In addition to visiting the Château, there are pleasant streets of half-timbered houses nearby (and an English tea-room), and much of later architectural interest.

POUL-FETAN

A preserved Breton village of yesteryear. During the summer all the old country crafts and customs are demonstrated with a programme of events every afternoon. In addition there are shops for local produce, a pottery, a bakery and a tavern where you can sample the local cuisine in the authentic atmosphere of an old Breton inn. Open end of March to end of September. (02 96 39 59 95)

ST-AIGNAN

This neat little village is well used to visitors having once accommodated the workers constructing the hydro-electric dam at Lac de Guerlédan. This connection with electricity is manifested in the **Museum of Electricity**. Just over the road, the attractive 12th century church contains some interesting examples of wood carvings, including a Tree of Jesse.

Electricity museum ©RDB

♦ST-NICOLAS-DES-EAUX

Situated on the canalised river Blavet, south-west of Pontivy, St-Nicolas developed as a staging post for canal traffic. Now it is a very pleasant waterfront with cafés, bars and restaurants. Take a trip on the river in the pleasure boat based here, or hire something smaller for independent enjoyment of the scenerey.

Stroll along the waterfront from the bridge and turn right opposite the lock to explore the back streets, including the Chapelle St-Nicolas with its beams dated 1534 and decorated with musicians, angels, dragons and fantastical lions.

Waterfront at St-Nicolas-Les-Eaux ©RDB

For another truly remarkable chapel, take the road to Pluméliau and just outside St-Nicolas, turn left following signs to St-Nicodème. (See Walk No.9)

La-TRINITÉ-LANGONNET

Lying just north of the D1 Guémené to Gourin road, La-Trinité-Langonnet is not to be confused with the town of Langonnet, near the abbey to the south of the D1.

La-Trinité church is noted for its stone tracery wall cupboard in the chancel. Walk across the road and follow signs (about 300m) to see the baroque fontaine in its elaborate setting.

©RDB

COMMENTS

Guémené-sur-Scorff does have some interesting old houses and they are well described in the TO's leaflet but some of them have been sadly neglected. For a spectacular arrival it's hard to beat the road through the Site de Castennec with its fabulous views and the descent into St-Nicolas-Des-Eaux, while the nearby Chapel of St-Gildas is a truly magical spot - well worth the climb down to it.

At Langonnet Abbey there is a very warm welcome for visitors.

The Nantes - Brest Canal

Near Rostrenen

Arguments for a series of canals linking the main towns of Brittany were proposed as early as the 17th century. The economic development of inland Brittany was hampered by the quality of the roads, and it remained in a state of poverty. Studies were commissioned, but financial concerns prevented any serious attempt until the end of the 18th century, when the strength of the British navy made terrestrial communications crucial for trade and military purposes such as the movement of troops and organisation of supplies. The Rade de Brest was particularly vulnerable to blockade. It was finally decided that a route from Nantes to Brest, part constructed canal and part canalisation of existing rivers, was desirable, in addition to a link with Lorient via the Blavet, and another north/south route from St Malo to the south coast. When Napoleon took an interest in the project, things began to happen. The first lock, one of 237, at Port Launay in Finistere was constructed in 1811. After the First Consul's departure, a canal company was established in 1822 and the canal finally opened along its full length in 1836.

It did, however, prove an expensive nightmare of construction with engineering problems and deaths among the workforce, in which prisoners of war largely replaced local labour as time went on. It was gruelling work, with much of the millions of square metres of stone and earth that had to be moved carried in sacks on men's backs.

The canal's original military purpose never really came to fruition, but barges transported slate, wood, and farm produce, despite the very high taxes levied on moving goods by this method.

The rapid development of the railways in the second half of the 19th century was a severe blow to the fortunes of the canal, although, with technical improvements to the locks, it enjoyed a brief heyday between 1890 and the outbreak of the First World War. After that, decline was steady as this slow and expensive method of transport, fell foul of the demands of the 20th century. The construction of the barrage at Lac de Guerlédan in 1920 effectively split the canal in two and significant economic activity was at an end.

Kilometre marker 265 near Glomel in the department of Côtes d'Armor, formerly known as Côtes du Nord.

In 1966, development for leisure use began and it is in this sphere that the canal is alive and well today. Walking, cycling, fishing and boating have provided a new lease of life for this 'blue road'. Today it is possible to walk the full length of the canal. Attractive spots for enjoyment of this very varied resource in central Brittany include Malestroit, where the Oust branches away from the canal, Josselin, where the route runs in front of the ramparts of the very impressive Château, and the Abbey of Bon-Repos, a beautiful country spot, where leisure boats are available.

Lock No.25 at Malestroit

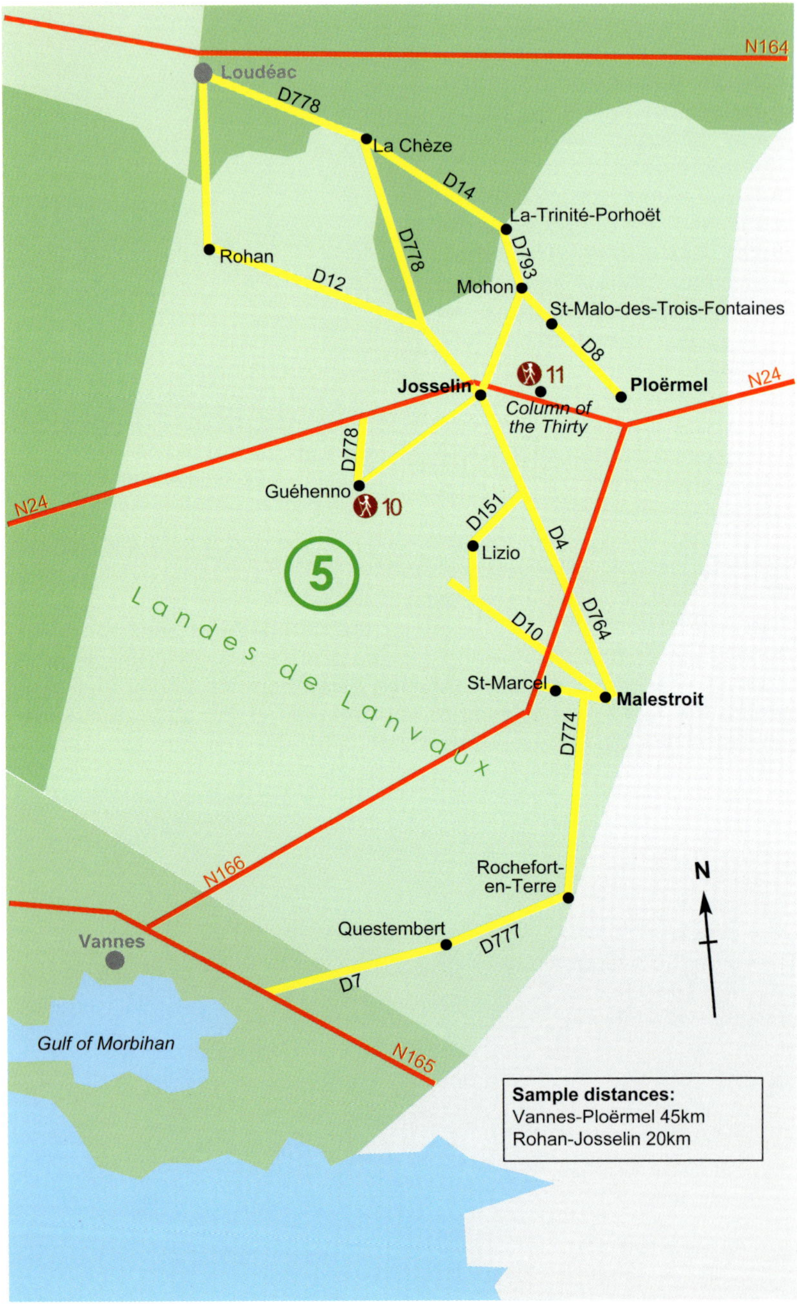
N164
Loudéac
D778
La Chèze
D14
La-Trinité-Porhoët
Rohan
D778
D793
D12
Mohon
St-Malo-des-Trois-Fontaines
D8
11
Josselin
Ploërmel
N24
Column of
the Thirty
D778
Guéhenno
10
N24
D151
Lizio
D4
5
Landes de Lanvaux
D10
D764
St-Marcel
Malestroit
D774
Rochefort-
en-Terre
N
N166
Questembert
D777
Vannes
D7
Gulf of Morbihan
N165
Sample distances:
Vannes-Ploërmel 45km
Rohan-Josselin 20km

5. The Argoat of Morbihan, Rohan to Questembert

It is almost impossible to ignore history in this area of Brittany. The powerful Rohan family, the War of Succession and the Battle of the Thirty have all left their mark. Castles, memorials, chapels and the moving Museum of Breton Resistance at St-Marcel can all be visited whilst exploring and enjoying the countryside. The fact that places of interest are concentrated in the northeast of the area is perhaps itself a reflection of Brittany's historical struggles with its neighbour France. Vannes seems to have been protected from the north by the empty moorland, the Landes de Lanvaux.

COLUMN OF THE THIRTY

©RDB

Memorial cross

At Mi-Voie, between Ploërmel and Josselin (just north of the N24) stands a column and a cross commemorating the Battle of the Thirty in 1351. The War of Succession over the dukedom of Brittany had been raging for ten years between the Montforts, supported by the English, and Charles de Blois. The two garrisons of Ploërmel and Josselin were on opposing sides and their commanders agreed to fight an engagement between thirty knights on each side. It was a terrible, bloody contest, with many deaths and not a man remaining unwounded, but de Beaumanoir was able to lead 18 English prisoners back to Josselin at the end of the day. The column records the names of the gallant participants in this ferocious encounter.

In the nearby village of St-Maudé stands a chapel, built in 1431 on the spot, it is said, where the knights killed in the battle were buried. (See Walk No.11)

La CHÈZE

©RDB

There are the overgrown remains of a 12th century castle here, including an underground passage, that you can explore at your leisure. It was built by Eudon II, viscount of Porhoët, whose grand-daughter married Alain V de Rohan. The accounts office and treasury of the vast Rohan estates were located at La Chèze until 1481, when they were moved to Josselin, the site of La Chèze having become less secure with the advent of gunpowder.

GUEHENNO

For a description of the famous calvary see Walk No.10, page 112.

♦**JOSSELIN** (TO 02 97 22 36 43)

©RDB

This pleasant town of old houses extends up the hill from the château, with a broad main street, rue Olivier de Clisson, leading to the Place de la Résistance, which on Saturdays hosts a market spreading into the surrounding streets. The Tourist Office is in a half-timbered building by the gates to the château and opposite is the excellent English Bookshop, run by Martin and Jennifer Green.

The château was founded by Guethenoc of the House of Porhoët in the early 11th century, and the settlement of Josselin was named after his son. Twice destroyed by Henry II (Plantagenet), the château was rebuilt and held by Jean de Beaumanoir in the 14th century wars against England. He took communion in the church before leading his Breton knights to the Battle of the Thirty in 1351 (see page 63).

The castle was owned for a short time by Olivier de Clisson IV, whose elaborate fortifications included nine towers and a huge keep. His second wife was Marguerite de Rohan and the château passed to Alain VIII de Rohan on Olivier de Clisson's death in 1407.

The earliest motto of the great Rohan family, found on a balustrade at the château, was 'a plus' (= sans plus – no-one superior). Despite suffering partial dismantlement by Francois II, Duke of Brittany, for the Rohans' siding with France against him, the château later became increasingly grand, with a huge logis building, probably from the time of Jean II de Rohan, when the family's support for the French throne was well rewarded.

In 1629 the keep and four towers of the château were demolished on Cardinal Richelieu's orders. There is a story that the Duke, Henri de

Rohan ignored the order and Richelieu himself arrived one day with the words 'Je viens, M. le Duc, de jeter une boule dans votre jeu de quilles' (skittles). The château fell into disuse in the 18th century, only to be restored from 1835 onwards. It served as a hospital for convalescing soldiers in the first World War and was occupied by the Germans in WWII. Today the château can be visited, together with the **Museum of Dolls** in the old stable buildings. This is a Rohan family collection from the last 125 years, with hundreds of exhibits.

The Basilica of Notre-Dame-du-Roncier

An account of 1666 tells how a labourer in the early 9th century found a statue of Our Lady among the brambles on the site where the church now stands. He took it home but the statue returned to its former location. The Bishop of Aleth authorized a new centre of worship there and the labourer's blind daughter recovered her sight, which led to its status as a place of pilgrimage. This story is told in the stained-glass windows in the church.

Romanesque pillars from the 12th century church survive, with unusual animal carvings, including a fox with a chicken. The tomb of Olivier de Clisson and his wife, which was mutilated in the revolution and later restored, can still be seen. A fine granite screen, bearing the M for Marguerite and the fleur-de-lis, separates the oratory from the choir, where the tomb originally stood.

Les Aboyeuses (barking women) of Josselin

This curious tale is a mixture of legend and historical record. According to the former, washerwomen of Josselin set their dogs on a female beggar, who turned into a 'figure of light' in the form of the Virgin, and for punishment cursed them and their daughters to bark like dogs. This is an awkward tradition for the Church – crude vengeance being rather out of keeping with the customary image of Our Lady!

In 1728 three children of a local family fell to the ground, barking like dogs (presumably a type of epilepsy). Their father took them to the statue of the Virgin and they were at once healed, as shown in a stained-glass window in the church. Later, epileptics came to the church in the hope of cures, and scenes of 'les aboyeuses' became common at the Pentecostal procession. There are stories of women in the 19th century, overcome with frenzy and howling, who were restored to calm, having been brought to touch the robe of Our Lady's statue (or a reliquary containing remains of the first statue).

Tourist Office ©RDB

LIZIO

©RDB

Though only a village and despite its rather scruffy appearance, Lizio has managed to become a 'petite cité de caractère' and offers visitors a variety of attractions, either in the village or the surrounding area. These include an **Insectarium**, open all year, inviting you to explore the fairy-tale world of insects, a traditional cider maker, a brewer of Breton beers operating from a former gold mine, an 'écomusée des vieux métiers' and an unusual sculptor or 'poète ferrailleur' who makes automata out of scrap-metal.

♦MALESTROIT (TO 02 97 75 14 57)

A lovely town on the river Oust and the Nantes-Brest Canal. In the centre, the church of St-Gilles has some interesting stone carvings around the porch and its stained glass includes a 16th century window dedicated to its patron saint. The half-timbered houses nearby display some delightful

©RDB

corbel decoration

wood carvings including a hare playing the Breton bagpipes.

Over a gateway in the Rue Heberdière, which leads to the canal, is a stone lintel carved in the three ancient languages that were required for novitiates to the Congregation of St-Pierre which was founded in 1828 in the former convent of the Ursulines. Today it is the Convent of Augustines with its adjoininng clinic. In the convent cemetery is the tomb of Mère Yvonne-Aimée de Jésus (d.1951). The sisters at the convent are happy to provide information for those interested.

On the outskirts of the town towards Guer stand the remains of **La Madeleine**, a priory of the monastery of Marmoutiers. Here in 1343, during the 100 Years War between England and France and the Breton War of Succession, was signed the Treaty of Malestroit, brokered (or imposed) by Papal envoys, thus preventing a battle that would have been fought in the region of Malestroit.

MOHON

The town's library is housed in the 'maison du sénéchal', which was built in 1653 by Julien Gaudin, the notaire of Mme de Sévigné, an influential society lady, whose letters have survived. One of his descendants later used it as a Chouan recruitment centre. Head out of town towards St-Malo-les-Trois-Fontaines and you come to the Camp des Rouëts, an 8th century embanked camp. It is thought that it was the residence of the kings of Brittany from Judicaël to Salomon (Rouëts - rois - kings). Next to it is a medieval motte. The two together, shaded by tall deciduous trees, are a great place for kids to let off steam.

Camp des Rouëts - the medieval motte ©RDB

PLOËRMEL (TO 02 97 74 02 70)

There is plenty to fill a pleasant morning or afternoon in the centre of Ploërmel. See the remains of the 12th century ramparts and admire the old houses, including the 16th century **Maison des Marmousets** and opposite it the former house of the Dukes of Brittany, parts of which date from the 12th century.

In the courtyard of an abbey now partly used by the Lycée Lamennais, an extraordinary astronomical clock works away inside a glass cage, and there is a small museum nearby.

©RDB

Astronomical clock ©RDB

The 16th century church displays a fine doorway with the apostles carved on the door panels and intricate decoration on the surrounding stonework. Inside, the early stained glass includes a life of St-Armel, the 6th century founder of the town.

The 19th century **Blue Chapel of Holy Mary of the Carmelites** (now an exhibition centre) has a unique atmosphere due to the blue glass of its windows.

To the north of the town is the **Lac au Duc** the largest natural lake in Brittany. Here you can swim, hire boats, enjoy water sports, and walk. There is a 3km walk through the famous Hydrangea Arboretum where you can see 400 varieties of hydrangea (hortensia), as well as a 16km circuit of the lake.

QUESTEMBERT (TO 02 97 26 56 00)

This market town is 23kms east of Vannes, and a good stopping point to replenish supplies or have a meal. In the centre stands an impressive market hall built in 1552 and restored in 1675, a more compact example than that at La Faouët and hemmed in by fine granite houses and shops. It was near Questembert (at Coët-Bihan) that Alain The Great was victorious against the Vikings in 888.

About 10 kms to the south east of Questembert on the road to La Roche-Bernard is a zoological park in the grounds of the château at Branféré, open every day in July and August but limited opening at other times (02 97 42 94 66).

♦ROCHEFORT-EN-TERRE (TO 02 97 43 33 57)

Rochefort-en-Terre sits on a rocky spur between two valleys, a situation that gave rise to a castle in the 11th century and the town that followed. Little remains of the castle except a few walls and dungeons but part of it was converted into a manor (visitable, 02 97 43 31 56) in the early 20th century by the American painters Alfred and Trafford Klots, whose works are on display there.

©RDB

The town is famous for its geraniums that decorate the streets and buildings, although these are exceptionally decorative even without the flowers. A mixture of architectural styles ranging from medieval to 18th century has created some beautiful street scenes with, apart from the occasional shop-front, few of the 20th century intrusions that are so common elsewhere. The church, Notre-Dames-de-la-Tronchaye, is tucked away down the southern slope of the hill, and consequently seems a little detached from the town centre. In high season the cobbled streets are likely to be very crowded with visitors, but this is a place worth seeing nevertheless.

ROHAN

Rohan (from the Breton for little rock) gave its name to one of the most famous families of the Breton aristocracy. Geoffroi, count of Porhoët, whose seat was at Josselin, gave land to his brother Alain, who, having first based himself at Castennec (See Walk No.9, page 107), then built a castle here at Rohan, - hence the name Alain de Rohan. The castle has since disappeared and is represented by an elaborate mural on the end of a house near the canalised river Oust.

Mural ©RDB

This area is the Port de Rohan on the Nantes-Brest Canal. Over the bridge is the Chapelle de Bon-Encontre, standing tall above the still water. Take a walk to the right along the towpath in the direction of Josselin to get a flavour of the canal.

Despite its historically evocative name, Rohan is rightly overlooked by most guidebooks - it has one of the ugliest mairies in Brittany.

Chapelle de Bon-Encontre ©RDB

ST-MALO-des-TROIS-FONTAINES

©RDB

Just a little bourg on the road from Mohon to Ploërmel but with not one but three fontaines, all in a row. They are dedicated to St-Mathurin, to the Virgin and to St-Malo. Legend has it that the water from one of them will never boil.

♦ST-MARCEL

Just outside Malestroit, St-Marcel was an important site of the resistance movement during World War II. Not far from an elaborate memorial to those who lost their lives in action against the enemy in this area, is the exceptional **Museum of the Resistance**. This contains a vast exhibition, both indoors

©RDB

and out, of war memorabilia, and detailed accounts of the events in June 1944 when a local armed Breton unit was forced to defend its territory against the Germans. The extent and variety of this museum's compelling contents deserves at least a half-day visit.

La TRINITÉ-PORHOËT

This sleepy little town on the side of a hill is certainly worth seeking out for its calm, unhurried atmosphere. The church is delightful, dating from the mid 11th century - a happy fusion of Romanesque and Gothic styles. The floor of the nave slopes with the hillside, down to the 13th century west door. There is a fine altarpiece donated by Mme de Sévigné.

©RDB

13th century west door

Down the hill from the church are some charming back-streets of cottages, while in the upper part of town, on the route de Goméné, is the 16th century chapel of St-Yves (open July and August, Tuesdays to Saturdays). In 1720 this chapel was used as a hospice for the poor, thanks to the curate Yves Lusse, who bequeathed his fortune for that purpose.

Chapelle St-Yves ©RDB

COMMENTS

Much of the TO information for this area is filled out with commercial padding and one needs to be selective. Some of the places on the tourist circuit are tiny and only worth visiting if you happen to be passing.

On the other hand, the powerfully evocative Museum of the Resistance at St-Marcel is excellent value and is great for children too - plenty of hands-on experiences and rides in period military vehicles.

Lizio, however, disappoints as a village, for all its accolades as a 'Petite Cité de Caractère, and many of its 'attractions' are not actually in Lizio itself at all.

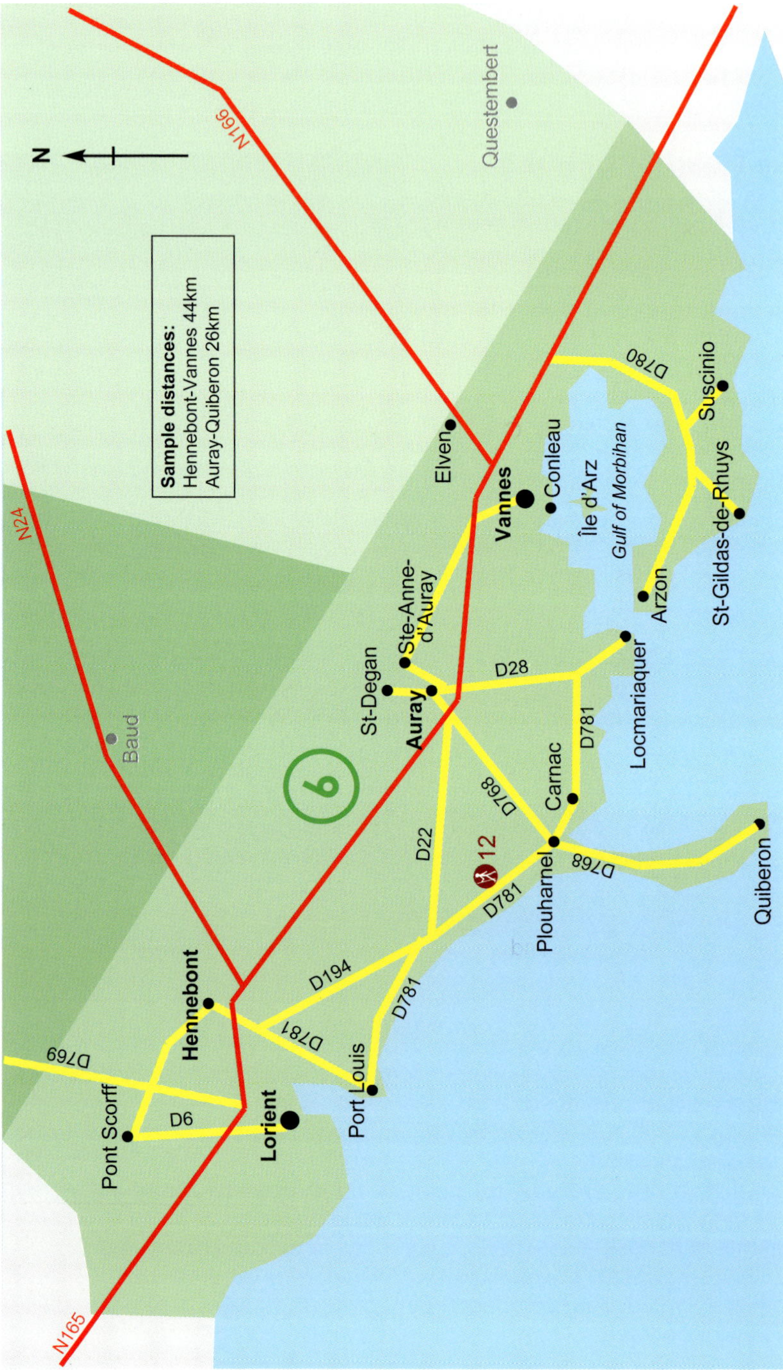
N
Sample distances:
Hennebont-Vannes 44km
Auray-Quiberon 26km
N166
N24
N165
Questembert
Baud
Elven
Vannes
Conleau
Île d'Arz
Gulf of Morbihan
D780
Suscinio
St-Gildas-de-Rhuys
Arzon
Ste-Anne-d'Auray
St-Degan
Auray
D28
Locmariaquer
D781
Carnac
D768
D22
12
Plouharnel
Quiberon
D194
Hennebont
D781
D769
Pont Scorff
D6
Lorient
Port Louis
6

6. The Southern Coast and Gulf of Morbihan

Besides the coastline, including the Gulf of Morbihan and its associated water-sports, southern Morbihan is noted for its megalithic monuments. Most people have heard of Carnac and the alignments there are truly amazing, but equally so are the neolithic cairn at Le Petit Point and the 'grand menhir' at Locmariaquer. There is also the medieval walled city of Vannes to explore and the gentle activity of Pont Scorff and its artisans.

ARZON

At the tip of the Presqu'île de Rhuys enclosing the eastern half of the Gulf of Morbihan is another group of neolithic monuments complementing those on the western peninsula at Locmariaquer as well as those on the island of Gavrinis. At **le Petit Mont**, a promontory jutting into the Atlantic, is a massive cairn dating from 5000 BC and displaying some artistic examples of neolithic stone carving. Wander round on your own or take a guided visit. Nearby is the **Tumulus of Tumiac**, otherwise known as the Butte de César because it was thought that it was from here that Julius Caesar watched the crucial sea battle in which he defeated the Venétès in 56 BC.

◆AURAY (TO 02 97 24 09 75)

Auray (not to be confused with Ste-Anne d'Auray) is a busy, bustling town on the hill above the river Loch that flows into the Gulf of Morbihan. It's worth seeking out the Tourist Office, housed in the Chapel de la Congregation, rue du Lait. This chapel was built in 1672 by Jean Bernard; the gallery copies the style of the Parliament building at Rennes. During the revolution it was used as a military court where Chouans (royalist anti-revolutionaries) and emigrés were tried before being shot at the 'Champs des Martyrs'. Auray is the birthplace of Georges Cadoudal, one of the most celebrated Chouans, and his mausoleum can be found in Kerléano, his home village, a short walk from the centre of Auray.

Port of Auray at St-Goustan ©RDB

©RDB

The Tourist Office will be able to show you two or three city walks. If you have time for only one, take the blue one, which leaves the lower part of Place de la République by rue du Château and descends to the old bridge over the river to the port of St-Goustan. Take a tour around the back streets of this old Breton port and return along the quay, where you will be amazed to find that Benjamin Franklin landed here in 1776, driven ashore by bad weather while making for Nantes, on his way to ask Louis XVI for French assistance in the American War of Independence. Since being restored, St-Goustan is a chocolate-box picture of sailing ships and half-timbered houses, amply provided with restaurants, cafés and crêperies. The schooner moored by the bridge is a floating museum.

♦CARNAC

Carnac is famous for its neolithic megaliths just outside the town. The principal alignments are those of Kermario, where there is a reception centre for visitors. Over the years **the alignments** have been attracting so many visitors that the ground around the megaliths has become denuded of vegetation and seriously eroded. This has meant that, unfortunately, for most of the year one is not allowed to wander among the megaliths at Kermario unaccompanied and you may prefer to experience one of the less frequented alignments such as those of Kerzerho near Erdeven to the west (see Walk No.12) or the alignments of Ménec directly north of Carnac, where there is an Archeoscope to help you understand what this is all about. Also worth a visit is the Tumulus at Kercado (from Carnac drive right past the alignmnets of Kermario and turn right).

In the centre of Carnac is the important **Musée de Préhistoire,** which on a wet day is much better value than traipsing around endless megaliths.

©RDB

CONLEAU

An island in the Gulf of Morbihan joined by a causeway to the mainland (to the south west of Vannes). It is from Conleau that boats leave for the Île d'Arz.

Île d'Arz ferry about to leave Conleau ©RDB

ELVEN

Just to the west of Elven, off the road from Vannes to Rennes, is La Forteresse de Largoët; which has the highest octagonal castle keep in France (14th century) and a restored 15th century round tower and a drawbridge. The castle is open from mid March to October, days and times variable according to season. (02 97 53 35 96)

GULF OF MORBIHAN (Mor-bihan = little sea in Breton)

The Gulf is a vast expanse of sheltered tidal water dotted with hundreds of islands, large and small, a veritable paradise for 'messing about in boats'. The coastline of the gulf either side of Vannes, and right round to the mouth of the gulf at Port Navalo is littered with boatyards and sailing schools. For a full list of all those providing boat hire, kayaking, sailing with a skipper and sailing lessons, all under the general heading '*nautisme*', contact the Vannes Tourist Office.

HENNEBONT

One of the oldest towns in the area, just up the river Blavet from Lorient, Hennebont has the remains of a walled town or 'ville close'. Just inside the twin towered gateway (Musée Tours Bro-Erec'h, open June to September) you can climb steps to a wall walk (Chemin de Ronde) that takes you down to overlook the river.

Les tours Bro-Erec'h (museum)

Don't leave Hennebont before visiting the **National Haras**. Here 70 stallions are kept from mid July to February: the rest of the year two thirds of them are elsewhere doing what stallions do but you can still admire the brood mares and foals in the park. All visits are guided but English is not a problem. The reception area has a well-stocked shop. Open: September to June, 9-12.30 and 2-6 but closed Saturday morning, Sunday morning and (outside school holidays) Monday morning; July and August 9am to 7pm.

ÎLE d'ARZ

This is the second largest island right in the middle of the Gulf of Morbihan and, although easily accessible by boat from Conleau (ferries hourly, even in low season), it is less developed than its neigbour the Île-aux-Moines. A coastal path goes all round the island, passing a tide mill, salt marshes, several good beaches and vantage points from which to view the rest of the Gulf of Morbihan. In the centre is a little town with a 17th century church and a bar/restaurant that is open all year.

♦LOCMARIAQUER (02 97 57 37 59)

On the peninsula enclosing the Gulf of Morbihan to the west is a collection of megaliths of awesome size, the Great Broken Menhir, which stood 20m high and weighs an estimated 280 tonnes, plus the Dolmen of the Merchant's Table and the Tumulus of Er Grah. This is a major site, whose excavation and restoration has done much to advance knowledge of the neolithic age. (Open mid-January to mid-December, times vary according to season.)

LORIENT (TO 02 97 21 07 84)

Built in the 18th century as the principal port of the French East India Company, Lorient takes its name from the first east indiaman built there, *L'Orient*. The city was largely destroyed in WWII and was one of the last places to be liberated. Today it's a modern city with little to recommend it other than its various port facilities. These include the Port de Plaisance (marina) where you will find the Tourist Office. Nearby you can visit the oceanography vessel **'La Thalassa'**, the Gare Maritime from where you can take a ferry to the Île de Groix, and the Port de Pêche. The **submarine base** (Base de sous-marins) is open for guided visits and even has its own Tourist Office, a portacabin, dwarfed by the vast, concrete WWII submarine pens.

©RDB

La Thalassa

PLOUHARNEL

Along the D768 out of Plouharnel on the way to Quiberon is the ♦**Musée de la Chouannerie**. Its WWII bunker is a warren of dark rooms housing a wide variety of written, pictorial and material evidence concerning an important epoch in Breton history. The Chouans (so-called after the screech owl's cry that was their signal) were a counter-revolutionary movement, pro-monarchy and staunchly Catholic, operating particularly in Morbihan in the late 18th and early 19th centuries. The atmospheric museum displays costumes, with their characteristic heart and cross symbols, weapons, paintings, documents and much else of interest that gives a true sense of the passion and commitment of these defenders of the old order. The connection with the Vendéen uprising of 1793 is made clear and also the disastrous defeat for Chouan forces by French revolutionary General Hoche on the Quiberon peninsula in 1795.

♦PONT SCORFF (TO 02 97 32 50 27)

La Cour des Métiers d'Art ©RDB

The heart of this little town is easily missed from the main roads passing through but dive off, preferably on foot, into the backstreets of old houses and you will find dozens of craft workshops. At No.8 Rue Prince de Polignac is **La Cour des Métiers d'Art**, where there is a vast display of art and objets d'art of all kinds for sale, much of it, though not exclusively, produced in Pont Scorff itself. In the adjoining courtyard are six independent workshops open to the public. Many other workshops are dotted around the town (leaflet available) and in high season most of them are likely to be open for visitors to watch the artisans at work.

To capture the charm of Pont Scorff don't miss the tree-lined Place de la Maison des Princes with its fine granite mairie. From the far end of the Place walk down to the old bridge over the Scorff. It stands on the line of the Roman road from Vannes to Quimperlé, although the bridge you see here now dates only from the 16th century. Little used since the construction of a new one in 1851, it owes its name, Pont St-Jean, to an almonery of the Hospitallers of St-John of Jerusalem that stood nearby. Three arches of the chapel dating from the 16th century are all that remain. Over the river, the Moulin des Princes houses **L'Odyssaum**, a museum of the wild salmon.

Take the D6 to Lorient to find the **Pont Scorff Zoo**.

©RDB

♦PORT LOUIS

©RDB

Entrance to the citadel

An old fortified town on a peninsula to the east of the mouth of the River Blavet. The fortifications of the citadel are Spanish in origin, dating from the Wars of Religion (1590-1598) when the Catholic governor of Brittany, the Duke of Mercoeur, sought aid from Spain against the protestant French king, Henry IV.

The buildings around the central parade ground of the citadel house two important museums. The **Musée de la Compagnie des Indes** tells the story of the French East India Company with displays of exotic goods traded from the Orient and from Africa and many scale models of sailing ships and life on board. The **Musée National de la Marine** has displays on rescue at sea and underwater archaeology on the passage to India.

©RDB

Musée de la Compagnie des Indes

The town centre nearest to the citadel is worth a stroll for its 17th and 18th century architecture and atmospheric cafés and restaurants, or take a walk along the ramparts overlooking the Blavet estuary with Lorient on the far side.

QUIBERON (TO 02 97 50 07 84)

The Quiberon Peninsula is a 13km long finger of land pointing due south into the Atlantic. The peninsula is approached through the town of Plouharnel (3km north west of Carnac) via the D768, which criss-crosses the railway all the way to the town of Quiberon at the end. In summer there is a train service with stops all along the peninsula - catch the train at Plouharnel (where you can buy a ticket at the Hotel Voyageurs or the Tourist Office) or from Auray.

From the harbour at Quiberon you can look out towards Belle-Île, to which there is a regular boat service from the Gare Maritime (next to the

Port de Pêche) as well as to the lesser islands of Hoedic and Houat. Along the front, hotels and apartments overlook a sandy beach. From Quiberon, take a walk back along the west side of the peninsula to see the Côte Sauvage, a rocky shore of inlets and turbulent waters - wonderful scenery but no good for swimming. If that is what you are after try the beaches further back at the Isthmus de Penthièvre.

©RDB

Cromlec'h de St-Pierre-Quiberon

At St-Pierre-Quiberon there is a reminder that you are not far from Carnac in the **Cromlec'h de St-Pierre** (signed just off the main road to the east), a circle of standing stones, perhaps a 100m in diameter, but sadly intermingled with houses, gardens and tennis courts. Not far away at Kerbourgnec is an alignment of 25 menhirs, and other neolithic monuments are to be found elswhere on Quiberon. On the west coast, opposite St-Pierre-Quiberon, the little fishing port of Portivy offers an opportunity for a stroll along the shore from the car park to the harbour and perhaps lunch at the waterfront café.

STE-ANNE D'AURAY

The elaborate church is one of the most famous Catholic shrines in Brittany, and a moving first World War memorial is also sited in the precinct. Ste-Anne d'Auray is a centre of pilgrimage, with its exceptional Pardon on July 26 attracting tens of thousands of visitors. Its importance was reflected in a visit from Pope Jean Paul in 1996. According to legend, the original church on this site was built after a vision of Ste-Anne twice appeared

©RDB

to a peasant, Yves Nicolazic, in 1623, urging him to dig up a statue surviving from a 7th century shrine in her honour. He found the statue and a new church was built. The statue itself was badly burned during the Revolution and its remains were included in the base of a replacement.

The current church was built in 1890 to provide greater capacity for the large number of pilgrims visiting the site. There is also a small museum, and the park contains statuary, fountains and La Scala Sancta, a 17th century ceremonial staircase.

The house of Yves Nicolazic, reconstructed in the early 20th century, can also be visited.

ST-DEGAN

The 'ecomusée' here demonstrates peasant life in the Pays d'Auray since the 17th century with a collection of cottages, complete with their furniture: the thatched cottage where a family lived with their animals, and the early 19th century 'longère' with its outbuildings, cellar, barn, well and bread oven. Take a guided visit in the afternoon or wander round on your own with an information sheet. In high season (July/August) there are daily demonstrations at 4 o'clock as well as a few all-day events on particular themes, with music and dancing.

SAINT-GILDAS-DE-RHUYS

The Irish monk Gildas is said to have founded a church here in the 6th century at a time when there was no other settlement on this promontory (and long before the Château de Suscinio). This early abbey was destroyed during the Viking raids on Brittany and then re-established by St-Felix in the 11th century. Many Romanesque elements from this

©RDB

period, not commonly found in Brittany, remain in the choir and transept of the current church, and ancient tombs include that of Jeanne de Bretagne (daughter of Jean IV, Duke of Brittany), as well as St-Gildas and St-Felix. There is also a treasury with ceremonial objects and reliquaries.

The famous Abelard, trenchant religious thinker and lover of Heloise, was abbot here in 1125. In letters to Heloise he describes the country and people as barbarous and wild, and says it's hard to recognise it as an abbey because of all the decorative hunting motifs. Not surprisingly, he became unpopular and was forced to flee a few years later. The church suffered fluctuating fortunes over the succeeding centuries with damage caused by lightning, neglect and decay, but the nave was restored in the 18th century. The Romanesque church of St-Gildas (under restoration at time of visit) remains open to the public.

♦SUSCINIO

A château at Suscinio existed as early as 1218 and it was to become one of the most important residences of the Dukes of Brittany in the 15th century. From here Duke Jean II set out on his last fateful journey in 1305, only to die soon after in Lyon when a wall collapsed during a papal coronation. During the Wars of Succession, the château was occupied by an English garrison and besieged by the great medieval soldier Bertrand du Guesclin. After the French Revolution the château fell into ruin, but it has now been restored to present a powerfully atmospheric experience of its former glory.

©RDB

Surrounded a moat, the château dominates the flat marshlands (marais) of the south coast of Morbihan, a position described in 1879 by the French writer Guy de Maupassant as standing 'all alone between two deserts - the land and sea.' A visit includes the huge rounded defensive towers and the residential logis with its large reception hall, upper ducal apartments and private chapel. The most striking feature of the interior is the range of well-preserved medieval floors with their decorative tiles, which are well worth seeing for their rarity value and the variety of their colour and motif.

Vannes, from outside the ramparts ©RDB

♦VANNES (TO 02 97 47 24 34)

Arriving on the outskirts of Vannes make for Le Port and park as near as possible to the end of the harbour. If you want to start with the Tourist Office, find it in Rue Thiers, an extension of the right bank of the harbour towards the town. The interesting part of town is through the 17th century Porte St-Vincent, the newest gate to the old walled city. Originally the water came right up to the city walls here and the gate was approached from each side of the harbour by a Y-shaped bridge. This area is now filled in (Place Gambetta) and accommodates pavement cafés overlooking the harbour. Inside the gate, the Rue St-Vincent contains town houses built for Breton parliamentarians when parliament was exiled here from Rennes following the 'papier timbré' revolution of 1675. At the top is the Place des Lices from where you can explore streets of half-timbered medieval houses leading up to the **Cathédrale St-Pierre**. Here is the tomb and reliquery of St-Vincent Ferrier, a Dominican monk and preacher from Valencia who, after a lifetime of travelling and preaching throughout Spain and France, ended his days here in Vannes in 1419, and was later canonised.

By the cathedral ©RDB

Opposite the west front of the cathedral is the **Cohue** (Breton word for market). The entrance is unappealing, plate glass between two medieval half-timbered houses, but the Cohue behind has over the centuries served as a market, a law-court and a parliament. It is where the Treaty of Union between Brittany and France was signed in 1532. It now houses the **Musée des Beaux Arts** (open all year).

'Vannes et sa Femme', 16th century corbel decoration, Rue Noé

The other important Vannes museum is the **Musée d'Histoire et d'Archéologie** (open mid May to end of September) in the Château Gaillard (rue Noé), displaying the permanent collection of exhibits from the palaeolithic to the Gallo-Romano period, including finds from Carnac, Locmariaquer and Arzon, against the background of a large 15th century town house.

There is much to enjoy in the old centre of Vannes, including cafés, restaurants, shops and a wonderful sense of stepping back into the Middle Ages. To return to the port, walk down behind the cathedral and out through the Porte Prison and turn right to walk along outside the ramparts, passing the ancient lavoirs and the Porte Potterne (both recently restored), and the Porte Calmont.

Back at the harbour, take a look at the old fishing boat in the first mooring on the left. The *Corbeau des Mers* (sea crow) carried 22 volunteers from the Île de Sein to England in answer to General de Gaulle's call to arms in June 1940.

Back in the car, drive down the right bank and out to the **Parc du Golfe** to visit the **Aquarium** and the **Jardin des Papillons**. The Parc is also where to find the **Gare Maritime** for a boat trip around the Gulf of Morbihan.

©RDB

Aquarium, Parc du Golfe

COMMENTS

In Vannes, the 'Cohue', an interesting medieval building with a history, is given over exclusively to the Musée des Beaux Arts. It is annoying that in order to see the building one is forced to take an interest in art, and pay the entrance fee to the gallery. Also annoying that the History and Archaeology Museum's important collection is kept away from the public for half the year.

If you love messing about in boats the Gulf of Morbihan must be close to paradise, and any TO can put you in touch with whatever guardian angel caters for your particular fancy.

WALK 1: Plestin-Les-Grèves

Length 8½kms	**Time** 3hrs	**Level** - difficult (steep path)

Location & parking: (this walk can be started at the Rue des Carrières on the sea front but, in summer, parking can be difficult.) Drive instead to Toul an Héry, taking the D42 out of Plestin towards Locquirec. The poorly indicated Toul an Héry is situated on the bank of the River Douron which divides Côtes d'Armor from Finistère. Park on the river front.

Refreshments: in Plestin, none on route.

Notes: the Sunday morning market at Plestin-les-Grèves must surely be the best in the Côtes d'Armor. Here you can buy your picnic or a pizza from the van or eat at one of the popular cafés.

1. Walk away from the bridge along the D42 following the shore. After 500m turn right into Place de Sainte Barbe where, until recently, the sea came up to the chapel dedicated to the patron saint of coastguard vessels. Go up the path to the left of the chapel, bordered by an ancient wall. At the top turn right and follow the lane past a few houses to its end. Turn left onto the footpath, open views to either side. Pass through a little wood of pine and juniper, keeping to the right on the yellow-marked path. After the wood, the path becomes a track and divides. Take the right track leading down towards a little farm where pigeons are bred. (Dozens can often be seen on the roofs.)

©PA

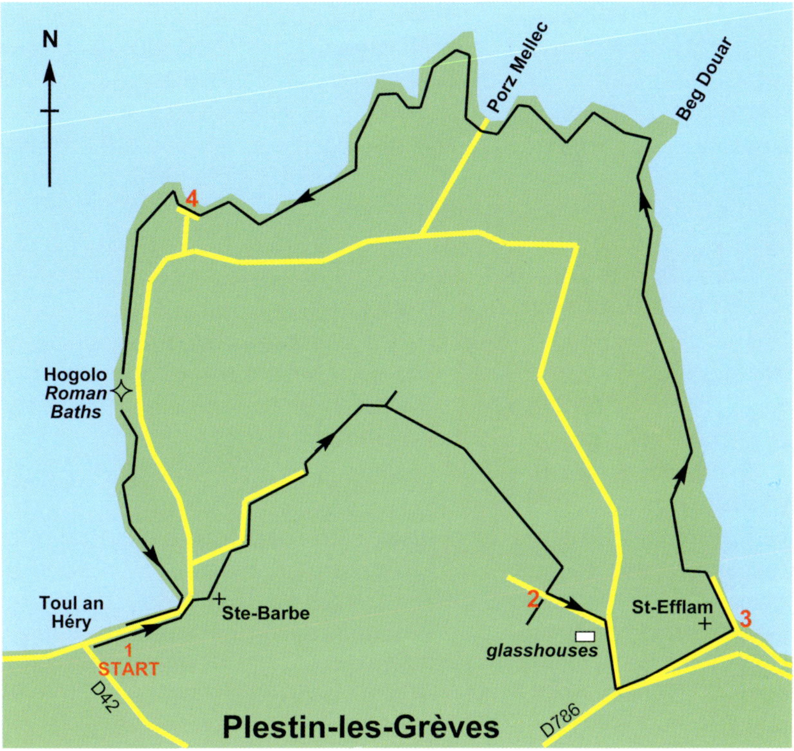

2. At the crossroads (where a marker points right to Traou-Dour) turn left up the lane, passing a group of greenhouses, to the road junction. Turn right, then, after 100m, turn left on the D786 towards St-Efflam. Keep to the left side of the road and go immediately down the car-free no-entry road to the left. The lane leads down to the sea, passing the chapel of St- Efflam high on the left. This can be reached by ascending the little path marked with a fleur-de-lys. Descend again by the wide stone steps to the fontaine, now neglected and denuded of its saints but still very sweet.

3. At the road junction, go left into the Rue des Carrières along the sea front. At the end of the road take the footpath climbing steeply onto the cliffs. Ignore all other paths and keep on this, the coastal GR path (red and white slash). The tide goes out an unbelievably long way in the huge, flat bay of Plestin and the sound of breaking waves and gulls can be heard all along the coastal path. (At the stone jetty of Beg Douar, benches afford a break and a sea view across the bay to St-Michel-en-Grèves and all along the coast to Trégastel.) Here and there, little footpaths lead down to the rocks and, further on, at Porz Mellec there is easy access to the sandy beach.

Crossing the road at Porz Mellec, continue on the GR where, behind a fence on the right, are wild cats which, when startled by dogs, scoot up the tall trees and stare down at you. Beyond the fence, where the path is now bordered by laurel and myrtle, look back at the layers of sand in the raised beach containing alluvial gold.

The path, running through what appears to be a perfectly planted rockery of tiny flowers, herbs and ivy, climbs steeply to a peak where the view opens out to include the pretty port of Locquirec across the wide river estuary ahead.

4. Still ignoring all other paths, stay on the GR which eventually arrives at a group of traditional Breton buildings. Turn right on the road and after 50m take the red and white marked path to the right, following it back down to the coast. Here, you can **either** take the path down to the beach and, when the tide is out, walk along the sandy river bed, **or** stay on the GR path that runs along the coast and rises to the left into pine woods. Just beyond the pine woods is the Roman bath of Hogolo, which can be reached from the river bed by giant pink granite steps. Though the herringbone walls of the Roman bath are now diminished to waist height, a terracotta arch remains intact and the layout of the baths can still easily be seen.

Continue on the GR path up-river and at the road, turn right and return to the car park.

WALK 2: La Roche-Derrien

Length 10kms	**Time** 3½hrs	**Level** - easy
Location & parking: La Roche-Derrien, 6kms southwest of Tréguier. Park anywhere near the square.		
Refreshments: in Pommerit-Jaudy and La Roche-Derrien.		
Notes: the walk follows the river Jaudy upstream through beautiful countryside, taking in several mills, two chapels, a château and a visit to the little town of Pommerit-Jaudy. The river valley is of metamorphised slate transversed with mineralised quartz veins carrying pyrites, gallina and spaylorite and small amounts of gold.		

1. From the square, descend the main road to the river. Don't cross the bridge to the Cheval Blanc but turn left to cross the river at the wooden footbridge, beyond which abundant trout gather and moorhens nest. Follow the path along the bank to the next footbridge, where a wild rose scrambles over the rails, and cross back. Go through a small caravan park and pass the kayak centre.

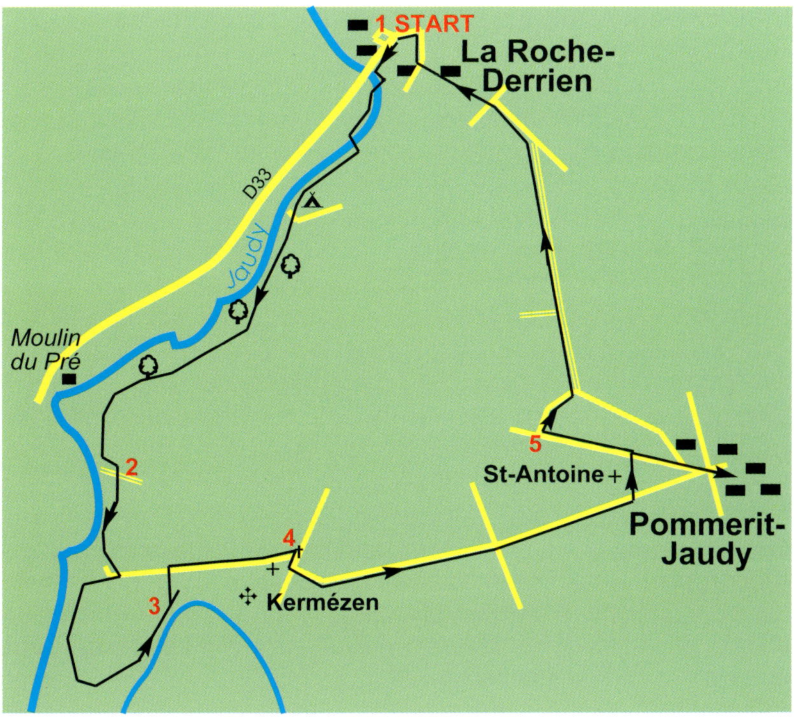

©PA

Cross the lane and follow the path into the woods. After 500m, the path leaves the woods and crosses the edge of a meadow and back into woodland diverging from the river, now bordered by poplars. The path comes back to the river at a little beach where two sections of river meet, having been divided to supply the Moulin du Pré on the opposite bank. Climb the easy steps to open country with the river flowing below through woodland and descend to a perfect picnic meadow bordering the river and looking back to the elegant mill house.

Back into low woodland, the path leads past the remains of a building, well-camouflaged now in ivy, and the river can be heard running through the race of another disused mill, the Vieux Moulin.

2. Cross the trackway onto a path, a deserted cottage on your left. Here the path narrows and passes through tall trees with willowy water meadows on your right.

After 500m, wide steps lead up to a lush grassy field which the path crosses to a track. Opposite, a barrier marks the edge of an enormous hydrangea (hortensia) nursery.

Turn right and descend the path which leads along the river and past the 'skeul pesked', or fish ladder which allows the trout to pass to their breeding grounds upstream.

Here, where the river is diverted to serve another mill, the Grand Moulin, the path leads along a bank, blue hortensias to the left and a neat plantation of poplars to the right and then joins the river again where, running fast and wide, it continues to supply yet another disused mill, the Moulin Kersaliou, now converted into a beautiful house.

Blackberries border the path which passes another gable end wall covered in ivy and the old quarry from which the stone was taken to build the mill. The path continues through the woods for 100m, where it forks.

3. Take the left fork up the hill, a track from the hydrangea estate joining it from the left, and keep on through conker heaven to the lane. Turn right into high, open country with long views on either side.

Pass the chapel of Kermezen on your right in its copse of chestnuts. Behind it, the 17th century Château of Kermezen offers 'chambres d'hôtes'.

4. At the forked junction, turn right and follow the road immediately to the left. ***(At the crossroads with an old, stone cross in the centre, you can, if you like, follow the path on the left back to La Roche-Derrien.)*** But otherwise, continue towards Pommerit-Jaudy along the Rue St-Antoine, passing a little shrine marking a source on your right.

Turn left along a footpath, passing the pretty chapel of St-Antoine, to the road junction.

Either Turn right along the road, cross the main Guingamp road at the roundabout and go straight on into the little town of Pommerit-Jaudy with its two bars both serving food, little shop selling tripe and boiled pigs' trotters, pizzeria and boulangerie. When well refreshed, go back to the roundabout, cross over and walk along the road directed to 'le reste de St-Antoine', back to point 5.

Or Turn left to continue the walk.

5.Turn right into a road marked 'Hent Gardenn Avalou' stopping to look at the noticeboard explaining how to make a dry stone wall like the one below it which was reconstructed in 1991.

The road passes a few modern houses then, where it bends to the right, follow the track opposite which divides immediately. Take the left fork and continue on this easy, sloping track with open country to either side, past another track to the left and down towards La Roche-Derrien which can be seen from the top of the track.

Turn left at the lane and continue to a road junction. Cross straight over and go down the footpath bordering gardens leading to a road junction in the town. Turn right then left to go back to the main square.

WALK 3: Kerpert		
Length 9kms	**Time** 3½hrs	**Level -** medium
Location & parking: in the village of Kerpert, park at the mairie.		
Refreshments: in Kerpert, none on route.		
Notes: a walk through hills and valleys, crossing the youthful Trieux and passing through woods and meadows. Wellington boots are recommended in wet conditions. (A notice board at the mairie shows a map of the Trieux from its source to the sea as well as local walks.)		

1. Go down the track ahead and at the fork follow the track to the right marked 'Fontaines'. The track, which is excellent for blackberries, descends gently at first, then more steeply through woodland as it rounds a bend and arrives at a junction. Follow the track to the left, ignoring the path marked 'Circuit de l'Abbaye', and continue over the Trieux which, though no more than an unimpressive stream, has carved out a wide bed of marsh and meadowland at this base of the valley. The track mounts gently, sloping fields now between it and the river, up to a road.

2. Turn right and after 100m right again in front of a stone cross planted with lavender. Pass the old bread oven on your left and the farm of Kergolou on your right and continue down the main trackway, keeping the group of modern barns on your left. At a forked junction, take the track to the right and descend into the valley and onto the tree-lined path straight ahead continuing down through the woods. In autumn keep a look out for the large variety of fungi that can be found in these parts. The path mounts again past a tumble-down building and a little path and continues, with fields to either side, into further woodland giving welcome shade in summer. Then it turns right onto a track and descends to a road.

©PA

3. Turn left and, passing a house on your right, leave the road for the track that runs beside a silver Christ on a stone cross. Descend the track through woodland and pass a small house on your left continuing on the verdant trackway over a stream and up to a group of houses where the grass of the track gives way to tarmac.

4. At the road junction, turn left in the little hamlet of Coldesquient and continue for 500m to a track on the right marked with the signs of three different paths (blue, yellow and the red and white of the GR). The track leads through open countryside and descends through beech woods with a view of a wooded valley to the right, then turns to the left

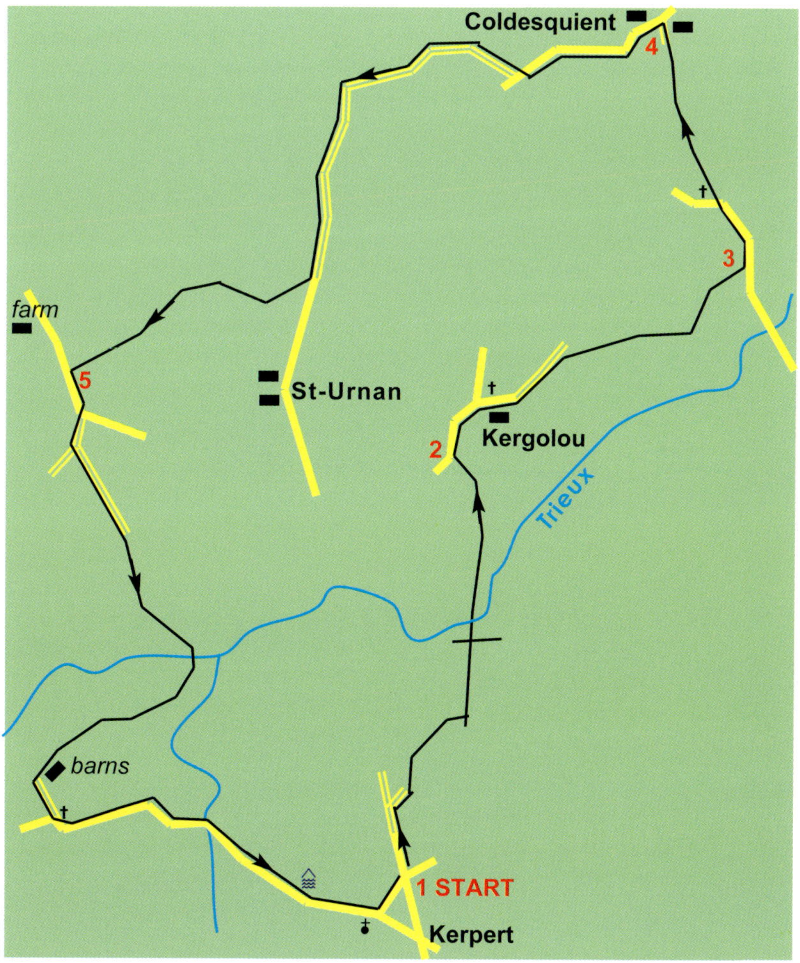

onto a track where it climbs again out of the woods and up to a ridge with long views on either side. To the left the dome of St-Gilles can be seen among the trees and, closer, the spire of Kerpert.

Before the hamlet of St-Urnan turn right onto a little path with a well-hidden yellow marker. Pass a couple of wooden home-made houses (and their goats) and descend the path through woodland of ancient beeches and pines, through splendid arches of holly and over a tiny stream at the bottom of the valley. Keep on the path as it mounts again through a field towards a farm on the right and arrives at a road.

5. Turn left and continue for 50m, then take the track to the right which forks almost immediately. Take the left fork and cross high open country before descending into the woods where the track narrows to become a path (shared at times with running rain water). Arriving at the marsh below, cross the stream, pass the barns on your left and, at the stone cross, turn left on to the road. Follow the road over another stream and uphill past the interesting but sadly neglected fountain of Notre-Dame with its equally neglected lavoir on your left and arrive at the attractive sixteenth century church of Kerpert, which is well worth a visit. To return to the mairie, continue to the junction and turn left.

©PA

WALK 4: Callac

Length 10kms	**Time** 3hrs	**Level** - medium
Location & parking: park at the station or outside the abandoned Hotel de la Gare.		
Refreshments: in Callac, none on route.		
Notes: a walk that leaves behind the sounds of the town and heads into peaceful countryside, passing on the way a Roman bridge, a reservoir and a ruined church.		

1. Cross the level crossing, climb the hill to the corner at the top and turn right onto the footpath running just behind the little cottage. Where the path diverges (the left leading to the farm) take the right and follow it onto a track. Ignore the path to the right with the red sign and go straight on along the side of a field. At the end of the track, turn right on the road. After a hundred yards turn left onto a track and descend, gently at first, then more steeply, into the valley. The dinky railway appears below and then the river. Follow the path through woodland. At the lane, turn right, cross another level crossing and rest, if you like, on the bench or explore the Roman bridge, its three arches with their domed roofs observed more clearly from behind.

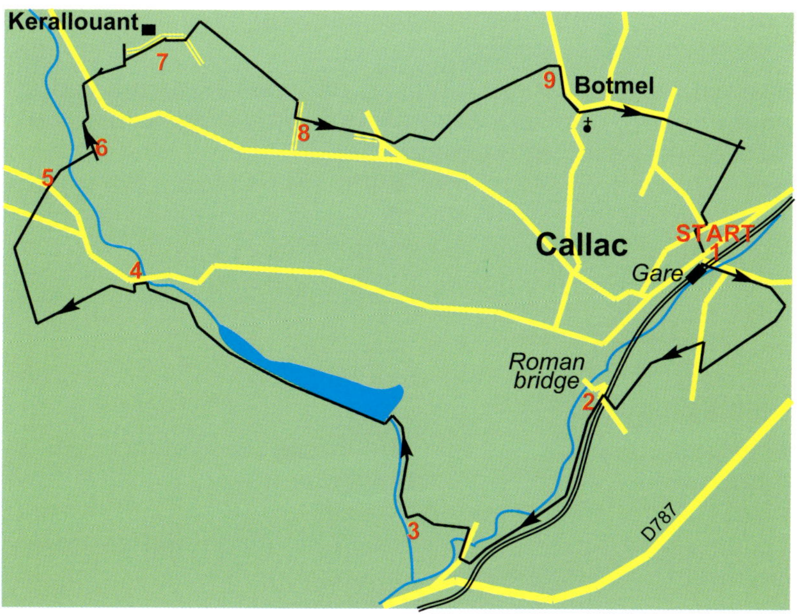

2. Cross the lane and continue along the path now running to the right of the railway. The trees give way to marsh and steps lead up towards the railway, but keep this side of it following the track that leads downhill away from the railway and arrives at a road, with the main Carhaix-Guingamp road to the left. Turn right over the bridge marked 'Hyeres', cross the road and go up the Rue de Noaledik opposite.

3. Take the path on the left immediately after the car park and follow it along the river, crossing a road and then keeping on the lower path which leads to the plan d'eau (reservoir). Turn left and cross the dam. At the end, turn right and follow the main path along the bank of the reservoir. At the head of the lake follow the sign, 'Circuit des 3 Rivières' and 'Tro Kallag', up the water meadow to meet the river (the Ruisseau de la Fontaine de Gervilly) at a bridge.

4. Go up onto the road, turn left and then immediately left again past a house. Turn right onto the track marked 'Tro Kallag' and continuing to just before the top of the hill, turn right. The shady path gradually descends to arrive onto a tarmac drive passing a few cottages. At the junction, cross the lane and follow the path immediately opposite at the side of a small shed. (This high-banked path, shaded with holly, ivy and yew and topped with deciduous trees, is a magnificent example of a 'chemin creux', the ancient and typical sunken footpath of Brittany.)

5. Cross the Lannion/Callac road and continue on the path now marked, 'Moulin de Kerallouant', as it descends more steeply, mounting and descending on wooden steps over a bank linking two fields. Follow the yellow sign turning right into a poplar plantation to arrive at a little stream joining a fast-flowing river. Cross the stream at stepping stones and continue along the bank, crossing the river at a wooden footbridge. Fifty metres further, the path meets a junction. (To return directly to Callac, turn right and follow the path back to the reservoir and walk into town along the other bank.)

6. Turn left, following the sign, 'Tro Kallag', the path bordering the channel diverted from the river by a weir. The path now climbs to the right away from the river. Cross the road and continue on the yellow-marked path which immediately appears to divide. Follow it to the right.

At the junction, keep to the path to the right, marked with a yellow sign, through a canopy of evergreens and out to banks of foxgloves, primroses and pennywort.

7. Pass the cottages of Kerallouan on the left and go right onto the lane leading downhill. At the corner, leave the lane and take the path to the left, just beyond a rambling box hedge. Follow the path as it runs parallel with the lane below and, arriving at a lane, turn right and, before the houses, cross immediately onto the yellow-signed path opposite.

8. Follow the path as it turns sharp right past a laurel hedge, descending past a cottage on the left to a lane. Keep going down the lane and turn left onto the yellow-marked path, which arrives at a group of houses and a lavoir restored with modern materials. Turn right on the road and cross it, then continue down the path at the back of the builder's yard. Arriving at a track, follow it to the left, signed, 'Tro Kallag'. After 50m where the path divides, keep to the right, following pink and yellow signs.

9. At the lane, turn right following the sign, 'Circuit des 3 Rivières'. At the top of the lane, take a little detour to visit the church of Botmel by descending a few yards into the lane ahead. The ruined church, on the left, is a haven of peace. (It is now possible to return directly to Callac by the lane descending past the church.) To continue with the circular walk, go back up to the road junction, turn right and follow the lane to a group of houses. Opposite the cottage, 'Loch Ar Cuidal', turn right and follow the road to the next junction. Go straight over the road and down the path, following yellow markers.

At a little cross roads, turn right. Follow the path to the right and arrive at a lane. Turn left, pass an old well on the right, and arrive at a junction. Turn right and immediately left into Venelle de Kermabilias. Descend to the road and the station opposite.

WALK 5: Bulat-Pestivien

Length 9½kms	**Time** 3hrs	**Level** - medium
Location & parking: Bulat-Pestivien is about 3kms east of the D787 Carhaix to Guingamp road, 7kms north of Callac. Park by the church.		
Refreshments: none on route.		
Notes: though Bulat-Pestivien is situated high on a granite foundation, the walks around it can be muddy in places due to the many sources, streams, lakes and marshes. Bulat-Pestivien means 'the head of three rivers'.		

1. Head out of Bulat on the Maël-Pestivien road. Just after the last house, turn left onto a track that passes a lavoir on the left and crosses a stream and follow it up the hill and onto open moorland. (View of Bulat's spire rising above the trees and, from the top of the hill, a spectacular 360° view of Breton landscape.) Continue on the track that curves to the right past another track joining it from the left. The track becomes a lane, passes several houses and arrives at a junction.

2. Take the right turning and ignore the path to the left, continuing on about 100m to a track that turns off to the left and passes through a tunnel of overhanging trees (more

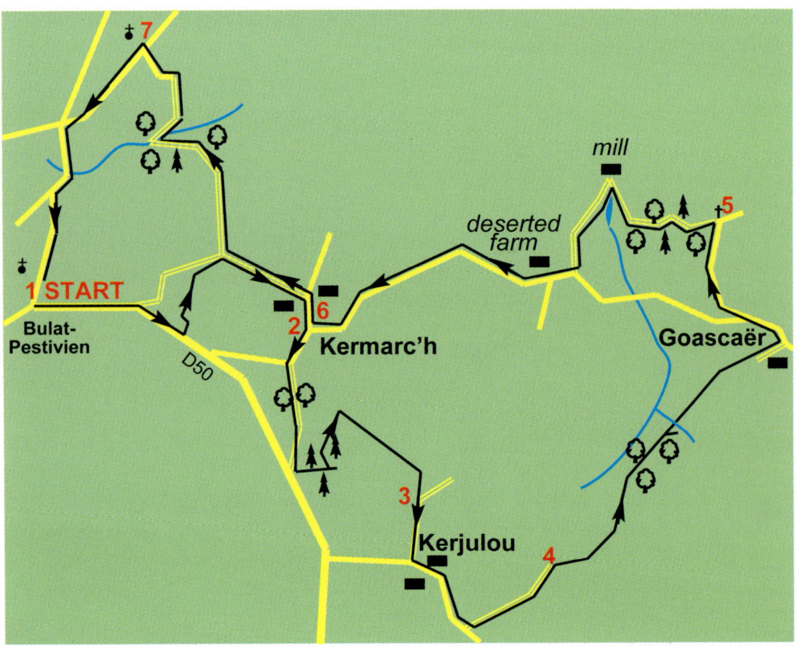

good views of the church behind) before leading down to a road. Turn left and then immediately left again onto a path that climbs through a wood of scotch pines. After 100m take the path to the left. (The yellow marker is difficult to find, but a yellow cross ahead indicates you should already have turned).

The path now winds through the woods and up over a bank to open scrub-land of gorse and broom. Turn left along the path with the bank to your left and open countryside to your right. Follow the path as it winds down again with views below and huge granite boulders dotted through fields and woods. Go over another bank and continue along the path on the other side. Turn through a gap in the bank and continue into a larch wood. The path descends gently and arrives at an old track at the bottom. Turn right and, with high tree-topped banks on either side, reach the junction of another track as you cross a little stream.

3. Turn right on the track towards the house at the top of the hill. Arriving at it, turn left into the traditional Breton village of Kerjulou. Before continuing on this road, take a little detour to admire the old village and especially the old stone carved with a chalice that once graced the fountain.

Back on the road out of the village, after 100m turn left onto a track that leads through open countryside.

4. At a corner where an enormous boulder has been clumsily cut turn right but do not follow the track. The path, marked with a yellow sign, leads along the bank at the side of the track, between rocks and oak trees to skirt a field with the bank now to the right. At the end of the field, past a magnificent beech on the bank, turn left onto a grassy path and drop down into the

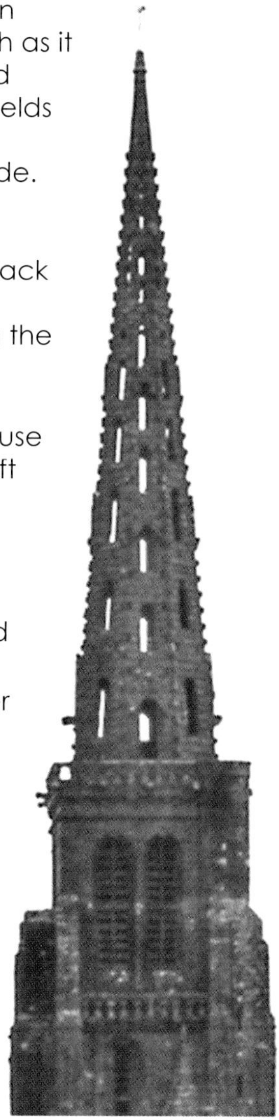

©RDB

wooded valley. At another large boulder - this one clean cut by nature - follow the path to the right and continue through the woods, a stream below to your left. At a fork, take the track to the left and cross the stream, marshland on either side. The track arrives at the hamlet of Goascaer, a pond with a tiny island below to the left. Turn left on the road and after 50m take the right fork.

5. Where the road bends to the right at a crucifix, turn left onto a track and follow it down past a plantation of young poplars and through ancient woodland to a lake. The track runs in front of the mill house and leat and climbs again away from the mill. At the road at the top turn right, pass the deserted farm and continue back to Kermac'h.

6. (same as 2). At Kermac'h, take a right turning, pass the cottages and return to the top of the hill with its 360° view. From here, either return to Bulat or take the right fork, marked with a VTT sign, and head for the original village of Pestivien, built long before Bulat.

As you cross the plateau towards the wood, pass a large boulder shaped like squashed dough and a long one marking the corner of the footpath and descend into the woods. (The spire of Bulat disappears and the steeple of Pestivien emerges into view). Follow the blue and red markers as the path snakes down the valley, squeezing past massive boulders and rising onto banks to avoid the mud from the plentiful sources.

At the bottom, the path crosses a stream which runs through marsh of great tufts of reeds and cow parsley, and continues through the woods where the sounds of the tinkling stream, birdsong and still the muffled bells of Bulat can be heard.

Follow the path as it bends to the left passing a house and turns into a lane. Pass a few more houses, the spire of Bulat now seen again to the left, and make for the spire of Pestivien straight ahead.

7. Cross the lane to the church. Call at the Presbytère next door for the key and, if you like, for a detailed analysis of the fascinating calvary in the leafy churchyard.

To return to Bulat, turn right on the lane as you leave the church and pass along the avenue of shady trees. Arriving at the road junction, turn left, then take the left fork up the steep hill back to the church of Bulat-Pestivien.

WALK 6: Locmaria, Rostrenen

Length 10kms	**Time** 3hrs	**Level** - medium

Location & parking: Locmaria is a tiny village on the outskirts of Rostrenen with an unusual 15th century church. To reach it from Rostrenen, drive up Rue le Hir at the bottom of the town and follow the road round to the left passing the Maison de Keramour on your right. Turn right at the cross roads and descend into Locmaria. Park by the cross below the church where the road forks.

Refreshments: in Rostrenen, none on route.

Notes: a walk mainly through woods and along the canal.

1. Down from the church, take the right fork, following the lane downhill, ignoring the track on your left and passing La Salle at the bottom of the hill. Continue to the road junction, cross over and onto a path beside a small house.

The conifer-lined path runs through mixed woodland where deer can sometimes be seen. A grassy field opens to the left and the path turns to the right where it becomes a track and then a lane passing a couple of houses, climbing a leafy hill and descending again, then passing the mossy wall of an old manor and arriving at a road junction.

2. Turn right, cross the road and turn left into the village of Kerbescont. Go straight over the road at the top of the hill and onto a track marked with a walking sign. After 50m turn right onto a track leading through woodland and over a stream (where white feldspar crystals can be seen in the

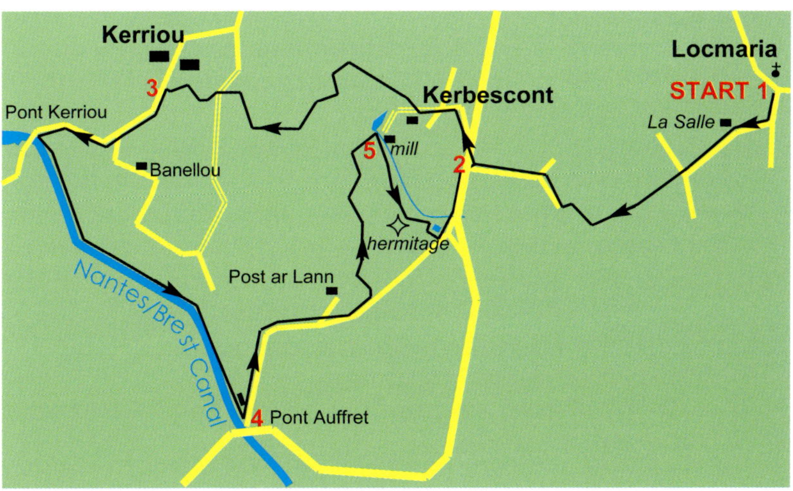

track). The track mounts again but two-thirds of the way up the hill, turn left into the woods on a small path marked (but sometimes obscurely) with yellow footpath signs. Drop down through the woods and over the little clapper bridge, then turn right and follow the path alongside the stream through the dark woods (still marked yellow but now with bright pink marks on trees and roots as well).

Locmaria ©RDB

On the right, tussocks of reeds in a swamp look like boulders in a stone circle and in the woods, trees sprout from huge boulders, all covered in moss.

The path slowly climbs through the beeches to meet a junction. Turn right and follow the path past more mossy trees and ancient banks. When you see the end of the woods approaching, turn right on the yellow marked path, cross a grass track and a bank, now following pink markers along the edge of a field and into the woods again.

Keep following the pink markers, crossing straight over a junction of paths. Immediately after passing a track on the left leading to a house below, the path forks. Take the right fork, still marked by pink dots, a stream running below on the left. Cross over an open clearing to arrive at a track bordered by a field beyond.

Turn left on the track, passing a pond and above it a house on your right and arrive at a road junction.

3. To the right is the village of Kerriou. Turn left and go down the hill, passing a sign to Banellou on the left, and arrive at Pont Kerriou, the bridge that crosses the canal. To the right of the bridge the canal widens to allow for boats to turn.

Do not cross the bridge but take the canal path on your left and amble the couple of kilometres to the next bridge at Pont Auffret, tall trees studded with huge balls of mistletoe lining the path.

4. Just beyond the little lock cottage turn immediately left up the hill, and, 100m past the turning to Post ar Lann, take the track on the left into the woods. Turn immediately left onto a path, marked with yellow, and keep straight on, the path running for a time beside an old sunken track on the left.

Where views of the valley open up below, the path turns left and heads towards two large pines but before reaching them turns left again back into the woods. Keep on the yellow marked path ignoring the temptation of various other paths. At a hollow at the bottom of the hill, follow it to the right. As the path, having circled through the woods and arrived at the top of the hill again, emerges, a portion of Rostrenen can be seen on the hill beyond.

Follow the path down the hill, the tall pines now on your right, and drop into a dramatic ravine, a wall of rock on either side, branches overhanging the path that climbs up and down until it mounts into more gentle woodland and the sound of the mill race can be heard preceding the view of the mill of Kerbescont below.

5. Turn right before the mill and follow the path along the base of the wood, the stream on your left. After 100m look out for the 'hermitage' on your right and take a detour from the path to climb up to it, first passing a little 'bassin' of source water edged with mossy stones. The hermitage was a cave converted for habitation and, though the massive rock that formed its roof has now been dislodged, the entrance stones where the door was fitted can still be seen and the cave can be entered.

If you decide not to take up residence, go back to the path and continue along it, passing a water treatment plant on your left and turning left onto a little road. Follow it to the left over the bridge and arrive at the main road. Cross the road and keep going to the left to arrive almost immediately at a sign to Keranna, pointing you onto the road to the right. Follow the road back the way you came to Locmaria.

Hermitage ©RDB

WALK 7: The Valley of the Gouessant

Length 6kms	**Time** 2hrs	**Level** - medium
Location & parking: from the D46 heading from Landehen to St-Glen, tum left to Moulin Gouessant. Follow the road to the river and park up the hill just past the red and yellow footpath marker on the left.		
Refreshments: none on route.		
Notes: the walk sets out along a wide flat valley, its tall trees, rich undergrowth and deep silence making this an attractive spot for wildlife. Herons can sometimes be spotted before they take off on silent wings. Return by higher farmland and villages to the reservoir, from where there is a choice of routes back to your car.		

1. Follow the footpath over a wooden bridge, up the hill and along a bank between fields before it descends through woods to the river. The river opens into a lake, actually a reservoir (so no swimming). Continue on the path as it skirts the lake and, at the end, tum left on the lane that leads round a corner and past a house on the right. You now enter the Pays de Montcontour where an interesting notice board gives information about the area.

2. Take the path that leads off the lane, keeping the next house on your right. Ignore the little path descending to the right, and keep going up into the woods. At the top follow the path as it bends sharply to the right and descend, passing beehives on the right, through the firs. The path now leads along the river again, this time on the left bank. After some distance the path passes the ivy-clad gable walls of a derelict building and arrives at a track which fords the river.

3. Cross at the footbridge to the side and, passing the water meadow, mount the track for 50m towards a farm, but before reaching it tum left onto the path running alongside the farm buildings. Descend the path back to the river, passing an intriguing ruin on the other bank with its decaying footbridge made of two rotting planks.

4. Keep on the right side of the river and, arriving at a track, follow it to the left along the river. Cross a little stream and where the track divides keep left, still following the river. Before the bridge, tum right, heading up through woodland, banks topped with trees bordering the path. At the junction, go right on the yellow marked path (leaving the red and yellow path to go left). After about 100m, before the entrance to a field, tum left up a grassy track which becomes a path, mounting through bracken, gorse and scrub oaks.

5. At the lane, tum right, passing through the little hamlet of Maubuchon with extensive views all round. At the next group of houses, go straight on and follow the pretty lane past abundant vegetable plots, apple orchards and beehives and cross a stream.

6. At the road junction of Les Boschiaux tum left and continue to the stone calvary set on natural rock in the middle of a crossroads. Turn right, passing through le Clos du Hêtre and la Huannière. Then go over the crossroads towards the Vallée du Gouessant. Descend the steep hill to arrive at the reservoir.

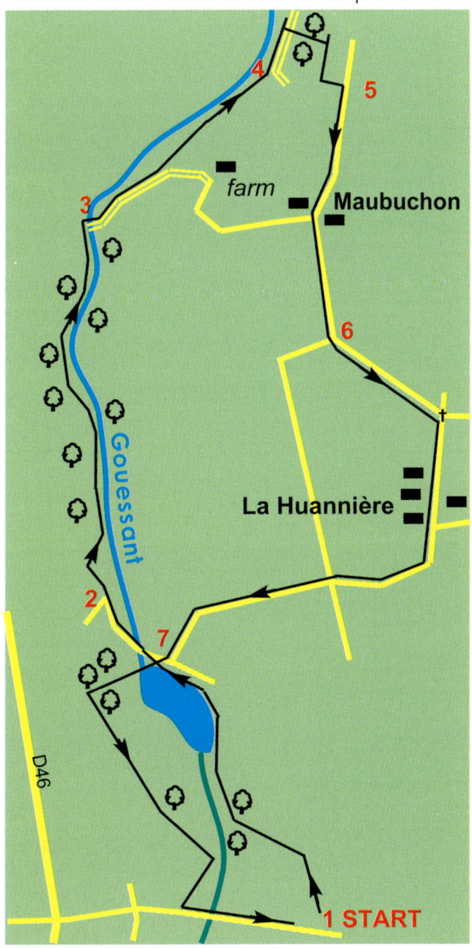

7. Here you can tum immediately left and follow your outward path back to the car or, more adventurously, follow the grassy path along the edge of the dam wall and go straight up the little path into the woods on the far side. Then follow the path through more rugged territory but don't cross the bridge when you arrive at the river again - stay on the footpath climbing through the woods of beech, holly and oak, seeing a house on the other bank and eventually coming out at the lane where you tum left, cross the river and come back to the car.

WALK 8: In Marion du Faouët country

Length 9kms	**Time** 2½hrs	**Level** - medium
Location & parking: centre of Le Faouët. Park near the 17th century Market Hall.		
Refreshments: auberge near the bridge (point 3), and another (in high season) by the Chapelle Ste-Barbe (point 2).		
Notes: this area gave rise to a colourful figure of the 18th century. Marie Tromel, known as Marion du Faouët, was a female 'Robin Hood' character, who led a band of robbers and highwaymen. She was hung in Quimper in 1755, aged 38.		

1. From the upper side of the main square (containing the market hall) in the centre of Le Faouët, take Rue des Halles. Cross over the cross roads, and go down the hill. The road becomes a wide track between banks and trees. At the bottom on the left is the base of a stone cross bearing a

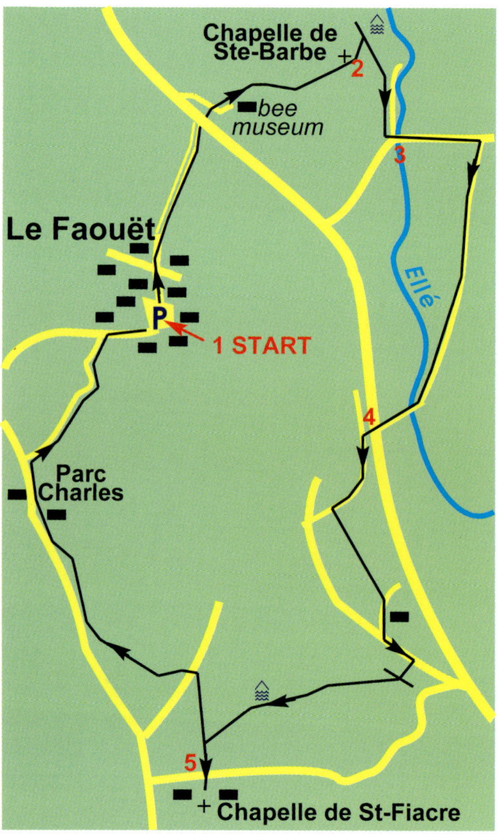

gothic inscription. Go through the tunnel under the main road and climb the steps on the other side. Follow the path over the little road leading (right) to the Musée de l'Abeille Vivante (bee museum) and go ahead uphill. This old pilgrim's way is quite steep and paved with granite slabs as far as two granite steps, after which it broadens out and continues to an open hill-top.

Continue ahead and through the low stone wall into the precinct of the Chapelle Ste-Barbe, which comes into view below you as you approach the balustrade. (With luck, the auberge on the left might be open for an ice-cream).

2. Go down the steps to the chapel, from the opposite corner of which a path descends diagonally through the trees. On reaching a larger cross-path, slightly to the left and straight ahead is a path leading to the fountain. Leaving the fountain, return to the cross-path and follow it to the left for about 600m, ignoring a path on the left signed 'Circuit du Chaos', joining a road and continuing right along it to a main road (D132) by a bridge over the river Ellé. (To the right on the main road is a shop/bar/restaurant.)

3. Turn left over the bridge and continue along the road taking the first turning to the right, signed to Stéroulin (meaning a stream where flax was processed). After a while a watercourse joins the road from the right, until turning sharply away by an old stone building, probably once used in flax processing. Follow the road over the river and through a hamlet to reach the main road.

©RDB

4. Cross over and follow the minor road on the other side to the left. Continue uphill and take the broad straight grassy track on the left signed 'Circuit des Chapelles'. When this reaches a little road follow it to the right through a hamlet to a main road. Here turn left for about 100m, then turn right between houses and follow the little road up onto the bed of an old metre gauge railway. Cross over this and follow the shady path slightly to the right. Follow signs to 'Fontaine'. This path climbs gently until arriving at a clearing with the Fontaine de St-Fiacre on the right. Continue on the path uphill and turn left at a T-junction of paths. At the road, cross to visit the Chapelle de St-Fiacre (open all year but may be closed from midday to 2pm). The chapel, which is famous for its fine jubé or rood screen (see below), has been restored to house additional items of religious carving in wood and stone. Don't miss the large communal 'four à pain' (bread oven) across the car park.

5. Retrace your path back to the T-junction of paths and continue straight ahead. Cross the road, and follow the old railway track bed to the left until it reaches another road. Do not join the road but take the footpath that follows the road to the right. When this eventually comes out onto the road, turn right and follow it through Parc Charles and after about 400m take the road on the right. This is tarmac at first, then a track, then a road again until eventually coming out at a T-junction in Le Faouët. Turn right to regain the starting point.

©RDB

WALK 9: Le Site de Castennec

Length 10kms	**Time** 2¾hrs	**Level** - medium

Location & parking: from the D768 between Pontivy and Lorient, take the turning to St-Nicolas-Des-Eaux. Before reaching the town take the turning on right signed to La Chapelle St-Nicodème. Park by the chapel.

Refreshments: in St-Nicolas-Des-Eaux.

Notes: chapels, fontaines, the Blavet Canal, the amazing Site de Castennec and a canal-side waterfront combine to make this a remarkable walk, mostly on the flat but with a few stiff climbs around Castennec. In the summer the chapels exhibit works of art under the 'Art in the Chapels' scheme.

1. Take the track that leaves the road in front of the chapel's magnificent tower and, passing to the left of the fontaine, descend away from the chapel. Follow this path as it crosses and re-crosses the stream until at the bottom you arrive on the towpath of the Blavet Canal. Here turn left and follow this towpath all the way to St-Nicolas-des-Eaux. The wide, peaceful Blavet meanders from side to side of a beautiful, deserted valley, its steep sides occasionally breaking into rocky cliffs almost hidden by the trees. After a while a railway line crosses the canal from the other side of the valley and then crosses back again as you enter St-Nicolas.

2. Arriving at St-Nicolas-des-Eaux, follow the waterfront to the bridge, cross it and take the canal-side road on the right for about 50m, leaving it by the footpath that climbs diagonally

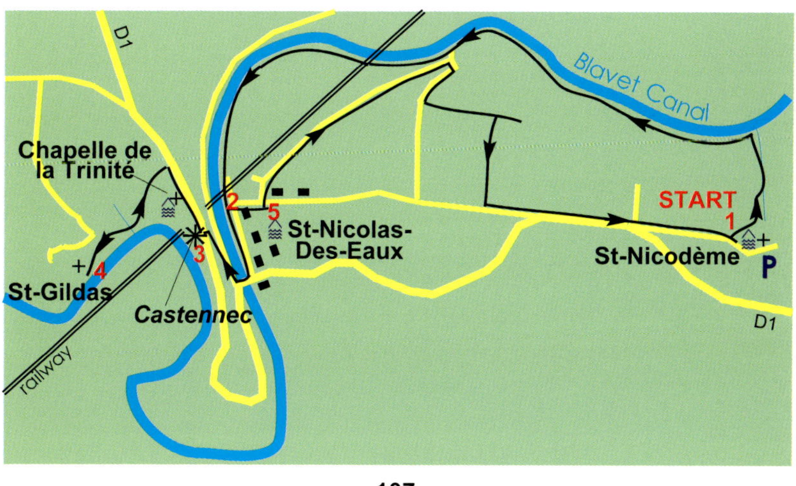

up the hillside to your left. Through gaps in the trees there are lovely views of St-Nicolas across the canal. At the top of the hill the path comes out onto the D1 main road. On the other side of the road, 50m to the right, is the stone built belvedere of the Site de Castennec. Climb the steps for a spectacular view. Castennec (Castel-Noec) was an important site in Roman times, under the name Sulis, situated on the main Carhaix to Vannes road. It became a feudal fortress in the territory of the ruling house of Porhoët whose seat was at Josselin. Alain, brother of Geoffroi, count of Porhoët, made Castennec his base before moving to Rohan at the beginning of the 12th century.

3. Leaving the belvedere, continue up the road to the Chapelle de la Trinité. There is a simple fontaine at the bottom of the park-like area before the chapel. Up the road from the chapel on the left, take the footpath that passes behind a house, end on to the road. Follow this down to the left between driveways. Leaving the houses, the path descends through woodland, crosses a stream and then rises briefly before descending again sharply by a large rock, to emerge on a grassy bank by the Blavet. But look behind you: an impressive rock-face towers above a tiny stone chapel built into the cliff (see page 52). The 16th century Chapelle de St-Gildas is said to occupy the spot where the saint, together with his disciple Bieuzy, created an oratory.

View from the belvedere at Castennec

4. Retrace your path all the way back to St-Nicolas-des-Eaux and, crossing the bridge, go along the waterfront. (If you have worked up an appetite by now, try the Crêperie Le Chalet.) Opposite the lock, take the Rue de la Libération, noting the stone well-head on the right, up to the Chapelle St-Nicolas. If the chapel is open take a look inside - it has some beams dated 1534 decorated with musicians, angels, dragons and fantastical lions.

5. Return to the Rue de la Libération and take the road opposite, Rue du Cosquer, taking the right hand road at the next junction, signed Le Guer. Follow this road all the way to the little road to the lock with its No Entry sign and here turn sharp right, following the same road uphill for about 400m, turning left along a farm track before the first house. After 500m in open fields take the track to the right and follow it to the road. Turn left, then left again (effectively straight on) where it joins the main road. At the next junction take the second road on the left, again effectively straight on, and follow this road all the way back to the Chapelle de St-Nicodème.

St-Nicodème, the patron saint of cattle, is said to have appeared to several local people asking them to build a chapel. In order to determine the right spot, they released some cattle and observed where they settled. Being cattle, they came to rest in this marshy quagmire. Hence the beautiful chapel of St-Nicodème in this unlikely spot.

©RDB

©RDB

WALK 10: Guéhenno		
Length 5kms	**Time** 1½hrs	**Level** - easy
Location & parking: the church at Guéhenno, which lies on the D778, about 10kms south-west of Josselin. There is a car park beside the main road, close to the church.		
Refreshments: in Guéhenno.		
Notes: very easy walk almost entirely on quiet roads and hard-surfaced tracks - a route suitable for pushchairs. Only the very short stretch in front of the Moulin de Château Merlet is a little rough. The last 500m is along a road that can at times be busy. The route passes a number of former mill buildings in watery settings.		

1. Walk away from the main road with the church on your right. Coming to the end of the road, cross straight over, following signs to the Chapelle St-Michel and yellow markers. The road climbs and takes a left hand corner to reach the top of the hill.

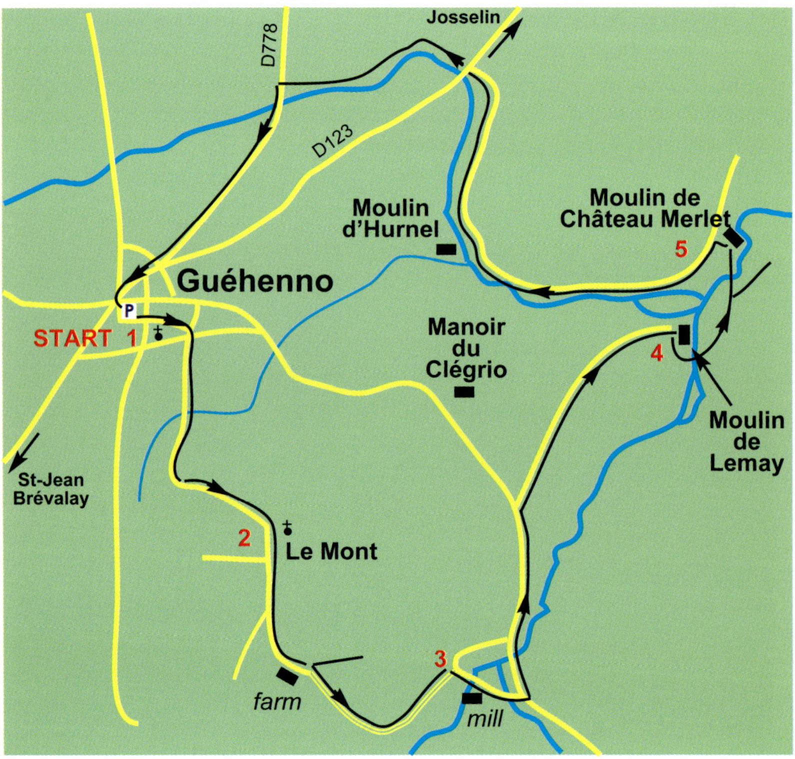

2. After admiring the views and the windmill, bear right around the chapel and continue ahead following the markers. The road begins to descend, and reaching a stone farm on the right hand side, you do not go straight ahead, but turn right down the wide track. On reaching the woodland at the bottom of the hill, the track swings to the left and continues ahead to meet the road.

3. Turn right on the road and cross the stream. Here is the first of the old water-mills. This one was built in 1878 and was working until 1940. Just past the old mill you reach a main road and turn left. The road passes the joining place of two streams and continues uphill. After about 500m, you reach a road branching off to the right, signed to the Moulin de Lemay. This road passes through a farm, after which you have good views across the valley on your left. The partially crumbling old farm across the valley is the Manoir de le Clégrio, which originates from the 17th century. The path now descends to the Moulin de Lemay, the mill with a turbine.

4. The path takes you around the right hand side of the building and continues under the trees. The stream is on your left, and where the track forks, you turn left to cross it on a wooden bridge (this is actually marked Propriété Privée, but underneath has been added 'Sauf Circuit des Moulins'). The

©JS

path now crosses in front of the Moulin de Château Merlet. The mill-wheel was on the far side of the house. The path now comes up to a small road.

5. Turn left on the road and continue through the wooded valley of the Sedon. The road is climbing slightly and passes yet another former mill, the Moulin d'Hurnel. This is now a very fine thatched riverside residence. Keeping ahead, you reach a main road. Cross straight over this to the track opposite - again a track beside woodland and the river. This eventually reaches another road, the D778, at which you turn left to return to Guéhenno.

The calvary at Guéhenno is not one of the most elaborate (that at Guimiliau in Finistère has more than 200 figures), but it does have a story. The original, dating from around 1550, was destroyed in the Revolution. The estimates for its repair by professional stone masons were far too great, so, some 60 years later, the local priest and his vicar decided to fix things themselves. They got the people to gather together all the fragments of the old calvary that they could find (it is said the revolutionary soldiers had played boules with the heads), reassembled them, re-carved them, and created others. The result was the interesting calvary you can see today - the faces are excellent. Look out for Jesse, the father of David, on the stem of the cross, and Mary Magdalene who carries a shroud. The cockerel, on its pillar in front of the calvary, represents Peter's denial of Christ. Behind the calvary is the ossuary - cast here in the role of Christ's tomb, the entrance guarded by soldiers.

©JS

WALK 11: Along the Ninian

Length 9kms	**Time** 2½hrs	**Level** - easy
Location & parking: in St-Maudé, near La Croix-Helléan between Josselin and Ploërmel. Park by the chapel.		
Refreshments: in Helléan, half-way round.		
Notes: a quiet walk through woods and open countryside, returning along the banks of the river Ninian. Some road walking.		

1. From the chapel at St-Maudé take the road opposite, follow it to a T-junction and turn left. Follow this road downhill, ignoring the turning to the left and the track opposite, until the road climbs to reach the village of La Croix-Helléan. Turn right just before the village sign. Follow this road downhill and where it swings left at the bottom, turn right onto a wide track with a red surface. Follow this track past the pond on the right, the house on the left and on into the woods. Follow the track round a sharp left hand bend, ignoring other tracks that form a crossroads here, and continue with alternating woods on one side and fields on the other.

2. Where the track eventually enters the wood, leave it and turn right along a lesser track that runs between the wood

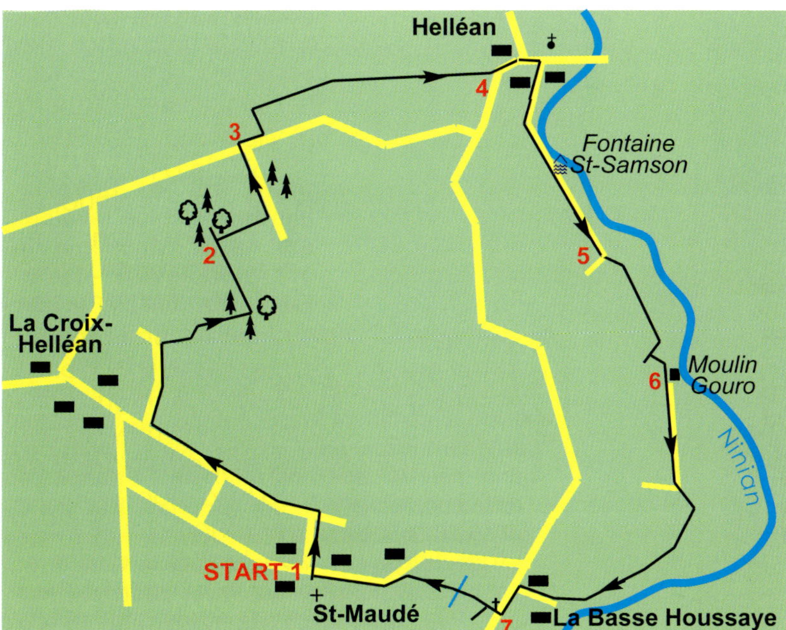

and an open field. Continue straight ahead until the track reaches a road. Here turn left.

3. At the T-junction turn right and then immediately left onto a track. After 50m, by the entrance to a field ahead, turn right and follow this track over the brow of the hill and down into the village of Helléan.

4. At the road turn left. Go downhill with the church on your left, turning right between houses just before the zebra-crossing. This little road is soon joined from the left by the river Ninian, where, on the right, there are a few seats in front of a cliff-face into which is set a shrine.

Continue along the road, past the 'Lavoir d'Antan' on the right and Fontaine St-Samson on the left. The river meanders away, comes back and meanders away again.

5. Where the road bends to the right uphill, take the track to the left, continuing roughly parallel with the river, but separated from it intermittently by water meadows, and with a wooded hillside on your right. Shortly after the track has turned away from the river, and over a little rise, take the turning on the left between a wood and a field that clearly belongs to a stables. Follow the track round the horse field and onto a little road by the Moulin Gouro, now a Pony Club.

6. Continue ahead on the road, past another coming in from the left, and where it bends sharply right and climbs, take the track on the left through meadows alongside the river again. Eventually this track leaves the river and, climbing, reaches the little village of La Basse Houssaye, an odd mixture of ruins and renovations. Follow the road to the right through the village, up to the T-junction and turn left.

7. Take the track on the right by the cross and, ignoring the track to the left after 50m, go down into the valley, over the stream and up the other side. On reaching the road, turn left and follow it back to the chapel in St-Maudé.

Chapel of St-Maudé (1431) ©RDB
believed to be on the burial site of the knights killed in the Battle of the Thirty (see page 63).

WALK 12: Erdeven

Length 8kms	**Time** 2½-3hrs	**Level** - easy
Location & parking: on the D781 leaving Erdeven in the direction of Carnac, park at the Alignments de Kerzerho.		
Refreshments: none on route.		
Notes: if you find the alignments at Carnac are open for guided visits only, this walk is a more than adequate substitute for those who prefer to explore megaliths at will.		

1. From the car park explore the alignments of Kerzerho. These are the westernmost alignments of the Carnac group, 195 megaliths in 5 rows, but unfortunately the road has displaced some of them. From a corner of the area, near the car park, a footpath leaves towards the 'Geants de Kerzerho'. This path shortly emerges in a series of little glades, each containing its own collection of giant stones, some standing, some lying, and with several smaller stones dotted around. Continue through the stones to a T-junction of paths and turn right, signed Mané Braz.

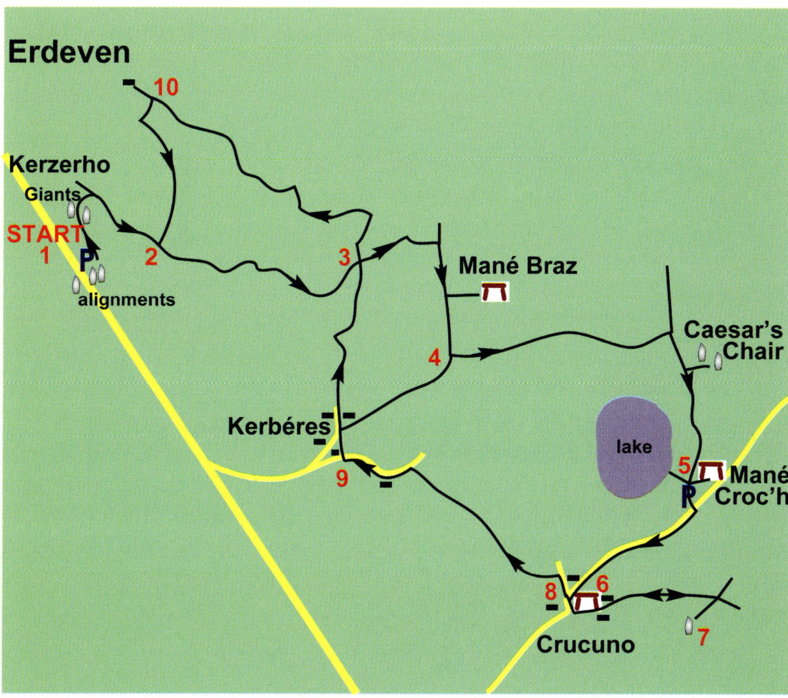

Giants of Kerzerho ©RDB

2. Where the path joins a track, follow it to the right. There are many hundreds of megaliths dotted around the pine woods and fields that border this wide, sandy track. Ignore any side tracks and continue to a crossroads of tracks.

3. Crossing straight over, continue to a T-junction of tracks and turn right. Shortly a path on the left leads uphill to Mané Braz, where there are four neolithic burial sites. The first is a dolmen comprising an entrance passage leading to four separate chambers. The second dolmen has just a single chamber and the remaining two, smaller dolmens have lost most of their roof stones. On leaving Mané Braz you will notice a line of megaliths on the opposite side of the path. Return down the hill and turn left to continue your walk.

4. After about 200m, take the track on the left signed to Mané Croc'h. At a crossroads of tracks turn right, still following signs to Mané Croc'h, and after about 150m, by a seat, take the path to the left to see 'Caesar's Chair'. Returning to the main path turn left and continue to a car park.

5. From the car park there is a path to the right that leads down to the lake (herons, sea-gulls and other bird-life), and a path to the left that leads up to the dolmen, Mané Croc'h, beside the road. Follow the road to the right to the village of Crucino.

6. Follow the road round to the left to see a massive dolmen beside a house. The roof stone is said to weigh 60 tonnes, the heaviest known.

7. Take the road that passes along the front of the dolmen house, following it between the houses and for about 500m to a crossroads and there turn right to see the cromlech of Crucino. Return to the dolmen house.

8. To continue the walk return to the road by which you arrived in Crucino, cross it and take the road that forks left of the modern house. After 100m take the earth road descending to the left and follow it swinging right uphill. At the end it becomes grassy and goes between gorse hedges, then crosses the top of a field and comes out on a road. Here turn left.

9. After the first house take the path on the right and when it reaches a road go straight ahead (signed Erdeven). The road becomes a track, leading to the crossroads of tracks at point 3 on your outward walk. Here go straight on, signed Keraveon. Continue on this track, ignoring signs to Kercadio.

10. When a house comes into view ahead, turn left (signed Kerzerho) and, following the path to the junction at point 2, turn right to repeat in reverse the first part of the walk back to the car park.

Dolmen of Mané Croc'h

SECTION C - TOPICS

(Numbers in brackets after places refer to areas given on the map on page 4)

• Islands • Archaeology • Museums
• Parks and Gardens • Children's Interest • Walking

©RDB

ISLANDS - Ferries and cruise operators

Bréhat / Sept Îles
Les Vedettes de Bréhat. 02 96 55 79 50 www.vedettesdebrehat.com

Gulf of Morbihan
La Compagnie des Îles - panoramic cruises leaving from Vannes, Locmariaquer, Quiberon and Port-Navalo. Easter to October and in school holidays. 0825 16 41 00

Navix - panoramic and gastronomic cruises from Vannes, Port-Navalo, Auray, la Trinité-sur-Mer and Locmariaquer. Easter to October and school holidays. 0825 16 21 00

Île aux Moines
Izenah-Croisières 02 97 26 31 45

Île d'Arz
Passeur de l'Île d'Arz 02 97 50 83 83 or 06 08 32 81 14

Gavrinis
Vedettes Blanche Armor - Larmor-Baden 02 97 57 15 27

Île de Groix / Belle-Île
La Société Morbihanaise de Navigation, Lorient
02 97 64 77 64 / 02 97 31 80 01

ARCHAEOLOGY

Plestin-Les-Grèves (1) The tourist office has information about local archaeological digs. The Thermes du Hogolo, the remains of a Roman bath on the Douron estuary, were only excavated in the 1980s. (See Walk No.1)

Plussulien (2) - neolithic axe factory. (See page 32)

Melrand (4) - on the D2 between Pontivy and Plouay. Ecomusée based on a deserted medieval village and its excavation. Houses reconstructed according to archaeological evidence. Open all year - times vary according to season. Individual or guided visits.

Gavrinis (6) - island in the Gulf of Morbihan - Neolithic cairn, the dolmen composed of richly carved megaliths - Open late March to early November, boat from Larmor Baden, southwest of Vannes.

Locmariaquer (6) - Great Broken Menhir, Dolmen of the Merchant's Table and Tumulus of Er Grah. Open mid-January to mid-December, times vary according to season. (See page 76)

Pointe du Petit Mont Arzon (6) - neolithic cairn, and Tumulus of Tumiac. (See page 73)

Mané-Vechen (6) - on the Ria d'Etel, near Plouhinec. 2nd century Gallo-Romano villa. Limited opening but usually July/August. www.plouhinec.com

Plussulien neolithic axe factory ©RDB

MUSEUMS and GALLERIES

These museums are open in season, and often at other times with reduced hours. Monday is a common closing day. The local tourist office will have up-to-date information about opening times.

Paimpol (1) - **Musée de la Mer** (Museum of the Sea) - the town's 500-year-old fishing industry.

Perros-Guirec (1) - **Musée de Cire** (waxworks) - French Revolution and Chouannerie.

Trégastel (1) - the **Radôme** telecommunications centre at Pleumeur-Bodou - museum with scientific games and a 'virtual world'.

Tréguier (1) - **Museum of Ernest Renan** in his timber-framed childhood home.

Corlay (2) - **Musée du Cheval** (Museum of the Horse) - at the castle.

Les Forges-des-Salles (2) - industrial history museum in old ironworking village.

St-Thelo (2) - **Maison des Toiles** - the story of flax.

Lamballe (3) - Maison du Bourreau (TO) contains two museums - **Le Musée d'Art Populaire** - history of Lamballe, including a model of the town in 1420 - Museum of the artist, **Mathurin Mehuet**.

Jugon-Les-Lacs (3) - **Ecomusée de la Ferme d'Antan**, St-Esprit-des-Bois - peasant life at the end of the 19th century.

Moncontour (3) - **Musée de la Révolution** - French Revolution and the resistance to it.
Museum of Theatre Costumes - portrays events of history from the 13th to the 20th century, through costume from stage and films.

©RDB

Baud (4) - **Cartopole** (Conservatoire Régional de la Carte Postale) - exhibition and sale of old and new postcards, mainly from Brittany.

Poul Fetan (4) - preserved Breton village with costumed inhabitants and artisans.

St-Marcel (5) - **Musée de la Résistance Bretonne** - tells the story and re-creates the atmosphere of the WWII resistance movement. www.resistance-bretonne.com

Josselin (5) - **Musées de Poupées** (Doll Museum) - dolls and toys of the Rohan family collection, in the former stables of the château.

Domaine de Kerguéhennec (5) (16kms sw from Josselin) - 18th century château with gardens and a sculpture park. Contemporary art, exhibitions, picture/video library, cafeteria.

St-Degan (6) - **Ecomusée de St-Degan** - illustrates peasant life in the Pays d'Auray since the 17th century.

Plouharnel (6) - **Musée de la Chouannerie** - a counter-revolutionary movement in the late 18th and early 19th centuries.

Hennebont (6) - **Le Haras National** - discover the horse in Brittany.

Pont-Scorff (6) - **L'Odyssaum** - discover wild salmon.

Lorient (6) - Port de Plaisance - **La Thalassa** - ocean discovery ship.

Brandérion (6) (6km east of Hennebont) - **La Tisserie** - discover weaving.

Vannes (6) - **Musée des Beaux-Arts** (La Cohue) - permanent art collection plus seasonal exhibitions.

Musée d'Histoire et d'Archaeologie (Château Gaillard, 2 rue Noé) - artefacts from the paleolithic (c.300,000 years BC) and later from Vannes and Gulf of Morbihan area.

Le musée aéronautique de Vannes-Monterblanc - a WWII hangar - aero engines, ejection-seats and various aeronautica - cargo plane 'Noratlas'.

Carnac (6) - **Musée de Préhistoire** - the world's principal museum on the period of the megaliths and Europe's third largest prehistory museum.

PARKS & GARDENS

Château de Rosanbo (1) - château gardens formally laid out with a large dovecote.

Château de la Roche-Jagu (1) – modern medieval-style garden, based on period when the château was built. Also pleasant walks in camellia wood and along the 'Chemin des Fontaines'.

Château de Kergrist (1) (on D11 between Lannion and Plouaret) - 5 hectare gardens open April - October (château interior guided visits at certain times).

Château of Bien-Assis (3) - a wooded park, reconstructed after the storms of 1987, retaining the 18th century planting systems. Includes an impressive avenue of oak and beech and a rose garden.

Quinipily, near Baud (4) - a delightful garden surrounds the statue of the Venus of Quinipily on the site of a former château. (See page 51)

Domaine de Kerguéhennec (5) (16kms sw from Josselin) - 18th century château surrounded by a botanical garden including a sculpture park.

Ploërmel (5) - the 3km **Circuit des Hortensias** by the Lac au Duc includes a huge range of form and colour in its hydrangeas.

Hennebont (6) - the central **Parc Botanique** - designed in the late 19th century and featuring plants from five continents as well as an arboretum, lakes and cascades.

Château de Kerambarh (6) - formal château gardens, also a liturgical garden, orangerie, kitchen garden and orchard.

Lorient (6) - the **Jardin Chevassu** - in a pretty valley setting with river and lakes and the remains of an old canal made by the Compagnie des Indes to reach the arsenal at Lorient.

CHILDREN'S INTEREST

This is not an area packed with children-focused attractions, except of the usual swimming complex/merry-go-round type. The following is a selection of places with potential interest for younger visitors. It is worth remembering that both north and south coasts provide plenty of free amusement for youngsters with the simple pleasures of the sandy beaches, and there are often organized clubs in resorts at very reasonable rates if some supervised play-time is in order.

The Pink Granite Coast (1) with its amusingly named and shaped rocks is fun for children – try a family walk along the Sentier des Douaniers from Perros-Guirec.

Pleumeur-Bodou (1) can offer the **Planetarium** and, perhaps for older children, the **Radome** and **Musée des Télécoms** which include mind-boggling technology up to the internet age.

Bothoa, St-Nicolas-du-Pelem (2) - **Museum of the Rural School** - an evocative re-creation of a school from the 1930s.

Poul-Fetan (4) - a village of ancient houses going about its business in 19th costume, with lots of interest for younger visitors.

La Chèze (5) - **Musée Regional des Metiers** - a fine collection of implements, tools and tricks of various trades, including the shoe-maker, weaver and blacksmith - demonstrations in season.

Saint Glen (5) - **Le Village des Automats** - a 'village' of often amusing clockwork and mechanised toys.

Malansac - south-east of Rochefort-en-Terre (5) - **Parc de Préhistoire de Bretagne** - although just outside the area of this book, it is worth mentioning this dinosaur park.

Branféré - off the D1, south-east of Questembert (5) - **Parc animalier et botanique de Branféré** - large zoological park with wide range of animals from around the world - visitors can feed and touch certain animals - spectacular bird displays.

Carnac (6) - **The Archeoscope** - may be an enjoyable experience - an audio-visual presentation about the megaliths.

Hennebont (6) **National Haras** (Stud Farm) - for horse-mad youngsters, this is not to be missed.

Vannes (6) - Parc du Golfe - **Aquarium du Golfe** - fish and amphibians from all over the world, from sea-horses to sharks. www.aquarium-du-golfe.com

WALKING

Section B of this book contains 12 circular walks (with maps and directions) spread over the area, but this only touches the surface of possibilities for active or relaxing walks.

Coastal walking is easy with the GR 34 almost encircling Brittany's shores. Pick it up at the Sentier des Douaniers on the Pink Granite coast or for cliff-walking near Cap Fréhel and Fort-la-Latte in the north, or discover the gentler inclines of the Quiberon peninsula and the area around Suscinio near the Gulf of Morbihan in the south.

Inland there is exceptionally beautiful river walking in the valleys of the Blavet and the Scorff in Morbihan and the Trieux and Leff in Côtes d'Armor. Wooded hills, spectacular granite gorges and a wilder landscape are readily available in the Argoat or interior countryside of the region. Walks from the Abbaye de Bon Repos, St-Nicolas-du-Pelem or the Landes de Lanvaux further south will provide this type of often dramatic scenery.

Town walking is frequently overlooked as a rewarding way of exploring history and architecture, and many tourist offices in the area can provide trail leaflets to give direction to wanderings in such treasure-troves as Pontivy, Vannes, St-Brieuc and Lamballe.

For waterside strolling, it is hard to beat the Nantes-Brest Canal, and there are often local circuits which avoid a return by the same path. The route right round Lac de Guerlédan is about 48kms, if you have a couple of days to spare for it – there are plenty of places to stay and find refreshments on the way.

©RDB

TOs usually have walking information, although not always in English and not always in great detail.

IGN Blue maps (1:25000) are readily available in newsagents and supermarkets as well as bookshops. These show walking routes, but not all are recent editions.

www.brittanywalks.com is a resource site for walking in Brittany, where helpful information and individual advice is always available.

INDEX

This includes all the main places mentioned in the text.
Main reference in **bold**.

other RED DOG books

Discover Brittany

Discovering the History of Brittany

by Wendy Mewes

A concise account of the history of this extraordinary region. It offers a clear picture of a complex subject through the presentation of people and places that have coloured events from pre-historic times to the present day. Colour photographs and line drawings illustrate many aspects of Brittany's historical heritage.

ISBN: 0 9536001 5 7 £8.99, 13.50 euros

www.reddogbooks.com

other RED DOG books

Explore Brittany

Walking Brittany

by Judy Smith

28 walks covering spectacular coast, hills and forests, varied water courses and traditional countryside. The text includes full directions and provides atmospheric accounts of places of interest on the routes - megalithic monuments, châteaux and sacred structures with their associated legends.

ISBN: 0 9536001 4 9 £9.95, 15.00 euros

www.reddogbooks.com

other RED DOG books

In the same series as this book

Finistere - Things to see and do at the End of The World

by Wendy Mewes

An introduction to the westernmost department of Brittany for visitors and residents alike, through a series of tours taking in all the main places of interest and quite a few of the less well-known attractions that Finistere has to offer.

ISBN: 0 9536001 2 2 £8.99, 13.50 euros

www.reddogbooks.com